Input in English-Medium Instruction

This edited book investigates the input provided by lecturers in English-Medium Instruction (EMI) to reveal the characteristics of both written and oral inputs in EMI settings and their pedagogical implications.

The book works on two assumptions: firstly, that field exposure to input is the prime mover of the teaching-learning process and secondly, that its quality is fundamental for the development of discipline-specific knowledge with particular reference to university settings. The volume is timely as it contains original research addressing both theoretical reflections and practical information on how content lecturers can enhance the effectiveness of their teaching practice through English including a relatively unexplored and increasingly relevant topic represented by the synergy between spoken input and written and multimodal materials.

Moreover, it provides insight for EAP teachers and EMI training professionals into how lecturer training programmes and activities can be improved by focusing on communicative functions and presentation strategies that can selectively address and improve students' mastery of disciplinary discourse.

Francesca Costa is Associate Professor of English Language and Linguistics, Department of Foreign Languages, Università Cattolica del Sacro Cuore di Milan, Italy.

Cristina Mariotti is Associate Professor of English in the Department of Political and Social Sciences at the University of Pavia.

Routledge Focus on English-Medium Instruction in Higher Education
Series Editors: Annette Bradford and Howard Brown

The series pulls together experts from around the world who are at the cutting edge of research on EMI within higher education. It presents a balance of research-oriented voices and evidence-based practical guidance for EMI implementation. Contributions will address the phenomenon of EMI from a range of international contexts.

The books in the series focus on contemporary developments in the field, providing concise, up-to-the-minute perspectives and examples to those involved in EMI planning and implementation. This series accepts proposals for books in two formats. The Routledge Focus short-form format is an excellent choice for shorter topics (up to 45,000 words) that reflect the quickly changing EMI research environment. When the topic requires more in-depth analysis, proposals for full-length monographs (up to 100,000 words) will be considered. Please clearly indicate which format you are planning when you submit your proposal.

Supporting EMI Students Outside of the Classroom
Evidence from Japan
Rachael Ruegg

Researching English-Medium Higher Education
Diverse Applications and Critical Evaluation of the ROAD-MAPPING Framework
Edited by Emma Dafouz and Ute Smit

Input in English-Medium Instruction
Edited by Francesca Costa and Cristina Mariotti

To access the full list of titles, please visit: www.routledge.com/Routledge-Focus-on-English-Medium-Instruction-in-Higher-Education/book-series/RFEHE

Input in English-Medium Instruction

Edited by Francesca Costa
and Cristina Mariotti

LONDON AND NEW YORK

First published 2023
by Routledge
4 Park Square, Milton Park, Abingdon, Oxon OX14 4RN

and by Routledge
605 Third Avenue, New York, NY 10158

Routledge is an imprint of the Taylor & Francis Group, an informa business

© 2023 selection and editorial matter, Francesca Costa and Cristina Mariotti; individual chapters, the contributors

The right of Francesca Costa and Cristina Mariotti to be identified as the authors of the editorial material, and of the authors for their individual chapters, has been asserted in accordance with sections 77 and 78 of the Copyright, Designs and Patents Act 1988.

All rights reserved. No part of this book may be reprinted or reproduced or utilised in any form or by any electronic, mechanical, or other means, now known or hereafter invented, including photocopying and recording, or in any information storage or retrieval system, without permission in writing from the publishers.

Trademark notice: Product or corporate names may be trademarks or registered trademarks, and are used only for identification and explanation without intent to infringe.

British Library Cataloguing in Publication Data
A catalogue record for this book is available from the British Library

ISBN: 978-1-032-19264-2 (hbk)
ISBN: 978-1-032-19267-3 (pbk)
ISBN: 978-1-003-25840-7 (ebk)

DOI: 10.4324/9781003258407

Typeset in Times New Roman
by Apex CoVantage, LLC

Contents

List of Figures		vii
List of Tables		viii
List of Contributors		ix

1 **"Input Matters" Also in EMI** 1
FRANCESCA COSTA

2 **Analysing Classroom Discourse and the Role of Productive Thinking in Teacher–Student Exchanges** 13
AINTZANE DOIZ AND DAVID LASAGABASTER

3 **Development and Application of the *Framework for the Analysis of Vocabulary Language-Related Episodes*** 26
HELEN BASTURKMEN AND JIYE HONG

4 **Features of Spoken Input Across the Disciplines and at the Interface Between English-Medium Instruction and Disciplinary Discourse** 40
CRISTINA MARIOTTI

5 **Materials Design for the Development of Subject-Specific Literacies in English-Taught Courses at University** 53
CYNTHIA PIMENTEL VELÁZQUEZ, MARÍA DEL CARMEN RAMOS ORDÓÑEZ AND VÍCTOR PAVÓN VÁZQUEZ

Contents

6 **EMI With a Twist: A Multimodal Analysis of Student–Teacher Agency in the Classroom** 66
   MONICA CLUA AND NATALIA EVNITSKAYA

7 **EMI Materials Development: Scaffolding Learning of Linguistics in a BA Programme** 82
   DARÍO LUIS BANEGAS

8 **Online Input and EMI Pedagogy in the COVID-19 Pandemic in Italy** 97
   FRANCESCA COSTA AND OLIVIA MAIR

9 **Input in EMI: Trusting the Process and the Journey** 116
   CRISTINA MARIOTTI

Index 126

Figures

3.1	Framework for the analysis of vocabulary language-related episodes (LREs)	30
7.1	Screenshot of session organisation	87
7.2	Use of graphic organisers	89
7.3	Use of bullet points	89
7.4	Completion activity	90
7.5	Video-based activity	90
7.6	Assignment briefing	92

Tables

2.1	An overview of the teacher-led questions normalised at 1,000 words	17
2.2	Closed questions versus open questions	17
3.1	Distribution of categories of focus by discipline	33
3.2	Sub-types of meaning-focused LREs by discipline	33
3.3	Sub-types of form-focused LREs by discipline	34
3.4	Targets of LREs by discipline	34
3.5	Sub-types of lexical choice-focused LREs by discipline	34
5.1	Model of language box	58
	Excerpt 6.1	71
	Excerpt 6.2	71
	Excerpt 6.3	73
	Excerpt 6.4	74
	Excerpt 6.5	74
	Excerpt 6.6	75

Contributors

Darío Luis Banegas is Lecturer in Language Education at the University of Edinburgh. He leads a core course on second language teaching curriculum and contributes to other courses on topics connected to motivation, identity and critical pedagogies. His main research interests are content and language integrated learning (CLIL), action research and initial language teacher education. He has published volumes on CLIL, action research, teacher education, and gender and sexuality in language teaching.

Helen Basturkmen is Professor and Major Specialism Leader in Applied Linguistics and Language Teaching at the University of Auckland, New Zealand. Her current research topics include EMI classroom interaction, EMI teacher education and teaching English for specific purposes. She serves on the editorial boards of English for Specific Purposes and the Journal of English Medium Instruction. Her most recent book is on the topic of linguistic description in English for Academic Purposes (Routledge, 2021).

Francesca Costa is Associate Professor of English Language and Linguistics at the Università Cattolica del Sacro Cuore of Milan. Her area of research focuses on applied linguistics, the teaching and learning of the English language at all levels of education (from primary to university) with a particular focus on codeswitching and translanguaging, Bilingual Education, CLIL (Content and Language Integrated Learning), ICLHE (Integrating Content and Language in Higher Education), EMI (English-Medium Instruction) and scientific English.

Monica Clua is a lecturer with the Department of Applied Linguistics and teaches research literacy and professional communication skills to students in the Faculty of Medicine and Health Sciences at the Universitat Internacional de Catalunya. She defended her PhD in 2021, which investigated interactional competence in EMI settings. Her research interests include disciplinary literacy development, English as a lingua franca and social/classroom interaction, through the perspectives of conversation analysis, membership categorisation analysis, multimodality and social semiotics.

Aintzane Doiz is Associate Professor at the Department of English and German Studies and Translation and Interpretation at the University of the Basque Country UPV/EHU (Spain). Her research includes English-Medium Instruction (EMI) and motivation in the acquisition of an L3 in CLIL and EMI settings. She has published widely in international journals and, together with David Lasagabaster, has edited several volumes in Multilingual Matters, Routledge, John Benjamins and Peter Lang.

Natalia Evnitskaya is a tenure-track lecturer and works as a teacher educator at the Department of Applied Linguistics, Universitat Internacional de Catalunya, Barcelona. Her research interests lie in two broad areas: (a) CLIL, EMI/ICLHE, TEFL, pre-service and in-service teacher education, classroom interaction, L2 interactional competence and multimodal conversation analysis and (b) CLIL, cognitive discourse functions (CDFs), disciplinary literacies, L2 learners' academic language proficiency, systemic-functional linguistics and legitimation code theory. She has widely published on these topics.

Jiye Hong obtained her PhD from the University of Auckland, New Zealand. She is Senior Researcher at the Institute of Educational Research, Sungkyunkwan University, Korea. Her research interests include policies, classroom interaction in students' acquisition of academic English and teacher education in EMI settings in secondary and tertiary education in Korea. Her recent research has appeared in the Journal of English for Academic Purposes (2020), Studies in Foreign Language Education (2022) and English for Specific Purposes (2022).

David Lasagabaster is Professor of Applied Linguistics at the University of the Basque Country UPV/EHU, Spain. His research revolves around EMI, CLIL (Content and Language Integrated Learning), attitudes and motivation, and multilingualism. He has published widely in international journals, books and edited books. Among others, he has co-edited "Language Use in English-Medium Instruction at University: International Perspectives in Teacher Practice" (Routledge, 2021) with Aintzane Doiz. He is the author of "English-Medium Instruction in Higher Education" (Cambridge University Press, 2022).

Contributors xi

Olivia Mair is a postdoctoral research fellow in the Centre for Higher Education Internationalisation (CHEI) and the Faculty of Language Science and Foreign Literatures at Università Cattolica del Sacro Cuore, Milan. Her research interests include English-Medium Instruction, Internationalisation of the Curriculum, CLIL (Content and Language Integrated Learning) and early language learning. She holds a PhD from the University of Western Australia.

Cristina Mariotti is Associate Professor of English Language in the Department of Political and Social Sciences at the University of Pavia, Italy. She has done research in the cognitive processes involved in the content-based learning of English and has published CLIL teaching materials. She has then expanded her interests to ICLHE (Integrating Content and Language in Higher Education), EMI (English-Medium Instruction), and the use of subtitled audiovisual materials in language teaching and learning.

Víctor Pavón Vázquez is Assistant Professor at the University of Córdoba (Spain). He is a member of the Committee for Language Accreditation within the national association of Rectors of Spanish Universities, current Director General of Language Policy and Director of the UCOidiomas language centre at the UCO. His current interests focus on research and development for capacity building of university staff to support the implementation of bilingual education programmes.

Cynthia Pimentel Velázquez graduated in English Philology and holds a master's degree in bilingual education. She currently works as a lecturer at the University of Córdoba, where she teaches in the areas of ELF and bilingual education. She is also Director of Language Accreditation. Her areas of expertise are evaluation of CLIL programmes and the development of pluriliteracies in materials design.

María del Carmen Ramos Ordóñez graduated in English Philology and holds a master's degree in bilingual education. She currently works as a lecturer at the University of Córdoba, where she teaches in the areas of ELF and Pronunciation of English. She has coordinated bilingual projects in bilingual state schools and has participated in several projects related to bilingual education. Her areas of interest are CLIL, teacher collaboration and Project-Based Learning.

1 "Input Matters[1]" Also in EMI

Francesca Costa

Rationale for This Book

English-Medium Instruction (EMI), that is, the teaching-learning of an academic discipline through the English language in non-English-speaking or English-speaking contexts where there is a large presence of international students, is a growing phenomenon throughout the world. This is partly due to the dominance of English as an international language in many fields of knowledge and partly to the need for many universities to become more international and attract both local and international students with courses and programmes carried out in English (Block & Khan, 2021; Bowles & Murphy, 2020; Dimova et al., 2015; Doiz et al., 2013; Jenkins & Mauranen, 2019; Lasagabaster, 2022; Macaro, 2018; McKinley & Galloway, 2022; Molino et al., 2022; Paulsrud et al., 2021; Wächter & Maiworm, 2014; Wilkinson, 2009).

The aim of this book is to investigate the input of teachers in the EMI field for three main reasons: first, because input is understood here as the *prime mover* of the teaching-learning activity; second, because input, ontologically speaking, entails a real didactic impact, as it can be adapted and fine-tuned by teachers to make it understandable and accessible to students; and third, because the input construct, which emerged from the field of Second Language Acquisition (SLA), can be a key to interpreting EMI teaching.

We shall start by describing the input construct as the *prime mover* in Aristotelian terms of teaching-learning, outlining the connection between the input construct in SLA and EMI and its role in these areas. We shall then focus on the function of both written input through the use of materials and oral input since:

> Not only do lecturers define terms, explain concepts, and give examples, but they also redress misconceptions, guide students through discourse, make sure that learners focus on what is important, and

DOI: 10.4324/9781003258407-1

establish meaningful interpersonal relations with them to facilitate the co-construction of meanings.

(Molino et al., 2022, p. 111)

The book rests on two references that in some ways represent its assumptions and starting points. First, David Bowie is thought to have made reference to input in one of his famous quotes. There is an analogy between the input that a singer puts into a certain song and how much of this input is used and reinterpreted by the listeners. The input of artistic yearning is seen both as a starting point and as a *prime mover*. Similarly, the input in EMI educational contexts is all that the learner (the learner user) is exposed to, which he or she will then understand while at the same time appropriating and reinterpreting certain elements of it. In some ways, these remarks also lead us to reflect on how sometimes those who provide the input are not fully aware of its importance and impact on the users. The idea that the input of teachers is varied, broad, and at times unconscious, from which each student can acquire, interpret and understand something, is fundamental. This characteristic of input, that is, the fact that it is the *prime mover* of the teaching-learning activity, is the first assumption on which this book is based.

The second reference, which has inspired the title of this chapter, comes from a 2008 volume: *Input Matters in SLA*, edited by Piske and Young-Scholten. The authors of this book seem to acknowledge that, although input studies have undergone alternate phases and interest over the years, the topic is and still remains a fundamental and underlying pedagogical intuition (see also Carroll, 2001) and an essential concept (Valentini & Grassi, 2017). The title also includes the acronym SLA, which clearly acknowledges that input studies arose from the field of SLA (and in some measure from psychology studies). Lately, input has been *rehabilitated*, in part because its relevance in EMI contexts is clear. As observed by Macaro (2018), "Tertiary-level EMI lectures are normally characterized by large quantities of teacher input." (p. 189). This book seeks to treat this concept more broadly by emphasising that input is also fundamental in EMI, especially since in such contexts there are a dual input and a dual processing that are mainly disciplinary but delivered through an L2 (English).

While it is true, as Macaro (2019) and Doiz et al. (2013) claim, that it was the applied linguists who were primarily interested in investigating EMI, it is likewise true that SLA can provide insights into both content and language (if we consider these as intertwined, as does the present work) and that multiple perspectives could enhance and better describe what happens in an EMI class. For example, Macaro (2018) identifies aspects of SLA interaction relevant to EMI contexts such as comprehensible input

(Vraciu & Curell, 2022), incidental learning and negotiation of meaning as modified interaction. These aspects will be taken up in the present work. Studies on EMI over the past 15–20 years have been based on constructs of Applied Linguistics/English Linguistics (i.e. systemic functional linguistics) but slightly less so on constructs belonging principally to SLA. In fact, EMI has been investigated in part from a spoken language point of view (Dafouz Milne & Núñez Perucha, 2010; Dafouz et al., 2007; Molino, 2015, 2017, 2018) by describing discourse-related functions, but less often from the point of view of input quality and of the input that comes from written materials, which presupposes a focus on the process of teaching and learning.

Apart from the conceptual framework considered (i.e. input studies), this book describes the input that is produced in EMI classes in various and diversified contexts, but above all, it analyses this input along two main axes: lecturer spoken input on one side and materials on the other (aspects already dealt with by Krashen, 1993). It is precisely the simultaneous presence of both types of input that contributes to the learning-teaching process. The input from materials has been little explored, and the synergy between spoken input and teaching materials has seldom been investigated in an EMI context. Coonan (2002) offers a categorisation that clarifies all the different forms that input assumes. Coonan describes both oral and written input by dividing these into input from the teacher, from classmates and from materials. As far as oral input is concerned, this can come from 1. the teacher (a presentation, questions and class management); 2. classmates (exposure, questions and interaction) and 3. materials (video). Written material, on the other hand, can come from a variety of sources: 1. the teacher (handouts, worksheets and glossaries); 2. other students (notes and exercises) and 3. materials (textbooks, authentic texts and CD-Roms).

The aim here is thus to reveal the characteristics of both written and oral input in EMI and their pedagogical implications, and at the same time to contribute to the fields of educational linguistics and applied linguistics through a construct typical of SLA. Referring to the ROAD-Mapping that Dafouz and Smit (2020) conceived of in the hope it could be useful for research, the present work falls within the fundamental field involving the description of (classroom) practices and processes (see also Sah, 2022).

Input Studies and Their Relevance to EMI

This section will provide a concise overview of input studies and the most important input presentation strategies in EMI contexts. We shall start from the seminal works in this area and then broaden the concept of input to include interaction and the negotiation of meaning, introducing the concept of input enhancement and the difference between incidental and intentional elements in teacher input. This chapter will conclude by emphasising the intrinsic relationship between language and content.

Simply put, input is the language and, in the case of EMI, the disciplinary content to which students are exposed. It can be written, as in the case of some materials, and oral, as in the case of lectures. When it comes to input, Krashen's work and his Input Hypothesis immediately come to mind. Krashen (1982) first distinguishes between acquisition as a subconscious process and learning as a conscious one. In his article on input, Sharwood Smith (1986) instead distinguished between comprehension and acquisition:

> I will focus on how 'language input' should be conceived of in the light of the different notions of *comprehension* (involving the decoding of particular messages that have been encoded in linguistic form) and *acquisition* (the creation of new mental structures which we call grammatical competence). The interpretation of input will, then, take two distinct forms: that which specifically involves extracting meaning from all relevant information perceived by the language user, and that which involves the mechanisms responsible for creating (or restructuring) grammatical competence.
>
> (p. 239)

This seems very relevant in EMI, where both language and content are to be comprehended. According to Krashen, the use of an L2 as the medium of instruction can provide learners with a large amount of comprehensible input. Comprehensible input is, in turn, considered a necessary factor for second language acquisition to occur (Gass & Madden, 1985; Krashen, 1982) even if it is not sufficient (as shown, for example, in the study by Roquet et al., 2020). In his input hypothesis, Krashen states (1982):

> The input hypothesis makes the following claim: a necessary (but not sufficient) condition to move from stage i to stage i + 1 is that the acquirer understand input that contains i + 1, where "understand" means that the acquirer is focused on the meaning and not the form of the message.
>
> (p. 21)

For Krashen, this input characteristic, that is, focus on meaning, can ideally suited to EMI. Subject matter input is also ideal for Krashen (1982), as he states in the requirements for optimal input:

> (i) *Comprehensible.* Subject matter teaching will be of use for acquisition only to the extent it is comprehensible.... (ii) *Interesting/relevant.* Subject matter may not always be interesting, but it is relevant. When

students are focussed on the subject matter, there is a very good chance they will be focussed off the form of the language it is presented in. Subject matter affords a good chance of meeting the "forgetting principle", of the student being so focussed on what is said that he is not aware of how it is said. . . . (iv) *Quantity*. Clearly, there is the potential of supplying great quantities of input this way. Subject matter teaching in the second language automatically reaches the pedagogical ideal of filling the entire class hour with comprehensible input.

(pp. 167–168)

Input becomes comprehensible if teachers provide this also "with the help of contextual and extralinguistic clues" (Ellis, 2012, p. 246), and thus use all possible channels.

More specifically, comprehensible input is elaborate and involves the use of presentation strategies. The input presentation strategies that have been investigated until now in EMI-like contexts are using repetitions, using examples, using synopsis/summaries, using definitions, explaining, reusing lexis, using synonyms, using paraphrasis, reformulating, asking questions, slowing down the pace of speaking, emphasising through intonation and articulating words clearly (Coonan, 2002; Costa, 2016; Costa & Mariotti, 2021), along with defamiliarising input strategies such as codeswitching and humour (Costa, 2017). To these should be added more strictly multimodal categories, such as visual aids, gestures and videos (Airey, 2011; Costa & Mair, 2022; Echevarría et al., 2008; Kasper, 2000; Morell, 2020), even if it should be noted that

> Comprehensible input is much more than simply showing pictures as visual clues during a lesson. It involves a conscious effort to make the lesson understandable through a variety of means. Communication is much more understandable through speech that is appropriate to students' proficiency levels. . . . Teachers will increase students' understanding by using appropriate speech coupled with a variety of techniques that will make the content clear.
> (Echevarría et al., 2008, pp. 79–80)

Long (1996) has somewhat expanded the theory of input by maintaining that both interaction and the negotiation of meaning are critical to make input understandable (Mariotti, 2007; Mariotti, 2016). Long (1996) extended Krashen's theory to posit that learning takes place through interaction and negotiation of meaning. The latter involves the resolution of communication breakdowns between speakers and the adjustments they make in order to understand each other. Long's Interaction Hypothesis (1996) thus suggests that interpersonal communication and interaction are also necessary in

EMI contexts if second language acquisition is to take place. This theory is also closely related to EMI since for Long there is an interrelation between focus on form and focus on meaning (Long & Robinson, 1998), which in some ways is similar to the relationship between language (form) and disciplinary content (meaning). Focus on form refers to moments within focus on meaning activities in which communication is focused on language. This book takes the position, however, that language and content are closely linked, and that language is a foundational and integral part of disciplinary knowledge (Costa, 2012; Stohler, 2006). Mohan goes even further (1986, p. IV) by stating, "It is absurd to ignore the role of content in the language class, just as it is absurd to ignore the role of language as a medium of learning in the content class."

Therefore, it is in continuous interaction and the negotiation of meaning combined with focus on form and focus on meaning that input is enriched and becomes relevant. "Input can be non-interactive in the form of texts that learners listen to or read. Alternatively, it can arise out of interaction, as when the learners participate in conversations" (Ellis, 2012, p. 205). A further concept that emerges from VanPatten's studies is that input enhancement can be considered a type of focus on form (Costa, 2012). Input enhancement is intended as an explicit technique to get the attention of students and thus favour learning. VanPatten (2009, p. 47) underlines that "[b]oth input enhancement and focus on form are grounded in the idea that work with formal properties of language for the purpose of fostering acquisition is best done if learner attention is simultaneously focused on meaning". All these theoretical references are bound together and seem to work in contexts in which the teaching process is focused on meaning, as in EMI.

A further element related to input studies and relevant to EMI settings concerns the concepts of incidentality (Basturkmen & Shackleford, 2015; Hong & Basturkmen, 2020) and intentionality. According to Hulstijn (2003), incidental language learning foresees a focus on meaning by the user who, incidentally, will capture linguistic elements without paying conscious attention to them. For example, Aguilar (2017, p. 726) states that "EMI implies that content – which is given in English – is the priority. Some incidental language learning is expected due to exposure but without any specific language learning goals" (see also Richards & Pun, 2022). In short, language learning could take place while a student's attention is focused on something else (content). Incidental learning is thus a process that takes place as a by-product of communication activities where the main focus is on content (Wode, 1999). In this way, the student would learn indirectly from both the teaching materials and the lecturer's spoken language. Intentional learning, on the other hand, implies an intentional focus on language. These two concepts historically belong to SLA, but they can naturally be applied not only to the language focus in EMI but also to the content focus. When it comes to EMI, where the main teaching focus is disciplinary content, it is important to analyse the linguistic aspect of input since, as noted earlier, if exposure to input is the basis of the learning-teaching process, then the quality of input from the linguistic point of view will also be fundamental. It is therefore important to describe this input and to understand how, whether incidental or intentional, it can be relevant to EMI. If the quality of the input is understandable, then it should facilitate both incidental and intentional learning not only with regard to content but also with regard to language. In that case, an EMI teacher will use more intentional input when focusing on disciplinary content while still providing more incidental input through his or her use of language and language materials. It is to be noted that in education the difference between intentional and incidental should be seen as a continuum. As Brown and Bradford (2016, p. 330) note, "The extent to which content and language learning are included as implicit or incidental aims of EMI courses is context driven, often depending on the personal attitudes of the individual EMI instructor or the discipline taught"; therefore, it can be useful to describe the characteristics of input in EMI settings and its educational implications also as a way of making lecturers more aware of their impact.

Structure of the Book

The book contains nine chapters: four of them are empirical studies and five are theoretical chapters including the introduction on input (Chapter 1) in EMI and the conclusions (Chapter 9). The contributions explore different geographical contexts: Spain, the UK, Italy and South Korea (see Pecorari, 2020 for an exhaustive discussion on the various forms of EMI), present very different methodological designs and instruments (interviews and stimulated recall, questionnaires, focus groups, action research, classroom observation, discourse analysis and multimodal analysis) and are in the form of short chapters.

The second chapter, by Aintzane Doiz and David Lasagabaster, is titled *Analysing Classroom Discourse and the Role of Productive Thinking in Teacher–Students Exchanges*. The chapter analyses spoken input, specifically questions and interaction by both professors and students, in an attempt to uncover productive thinking in their exchanges. The sample of analysis includes eight EMI history lectures of two hours each, with the results showing that lecturers try to elicit productive thinking through the use of questions but that interaction between students and lecturers is still limited. In light of these results, the pedagogical implications are discussed.

The third chapter is by Helen Basturkmen and Jiye Hong and is titled *Development and Application of the Framework for the Analysis of Vocabulary Language-Related Episodes*. The chapter focuses on spoken input, particularly LREs (Language-Related Episodes), which offer an excellent starting point for focusing on form in meaning-based activities. The study illustrates examples of LREs in accounting and mathematics in higher education classes in South Korea by means of a framework and discusses LREs involving vocabulary by providing suggestions on how LREs can be implemented.

The chapter *Features of Spoken Input Across the Disciplines and at the Interface Between English-Medium Instruction and Disciplinary Discourse* by Cristina Mariotti involves features that characterise spoken input regardless of the discipline being taught and investigates what features are discipline-specific. The aim of the chapter is to help lecturers from all fields of expertise improve their pedagogical knowledge and metalinguistic awareness of the features of their disciplinary discourse and to learn about (co)construction strategies in order to make the most out of their lecturing activity.

The chapter titled *Materials Design for the Development of Subject-Specific Literacies in English-Taught Courses at the University* by Cynthia Pimentel Velázquez, María del Carmen Ramos Ordóñez and Víctor Pavón Vázquez focuses on written input in the form of disciplinary academic language in EMI and how this can be developed through materials design. Subject-specific literacies are indicators of academic failure if they are not developed correctly. The chapter identifies effective features of EMI materials and offers practical suggestions on how to develop them.

The chapter titled *EMI With a Twist: A Multimodal Analysis of Student–Teacher Agency in the Classroom* by Monica Clua and Natalia Evnitskaya focuses on how students display their agency and co-construct classroom discourse with their lecturer. Data are derived from a multimodal and conversation analysis, membership categorisation analysis and positioning analysis of a lesson on dentistry materials with students having an advanced level of English. Results show role reversals with students eliciting the teacher's spoken input and co-constructing subject knowledge.

The seventh chapter, by Darío Luis Banegas, is titled *EMI Materials Development: Scaffolding Learning of Linguistics in a BA Programme*. It examines written input and the design and choice of materials for a linguistics course in a UK university with an international student body (Omani). The data was collected from group discussions and document analysis. The results show an integration between language and content which may provide useful advice for other teachers.

Finally, the chapter *Online Input and EMI Pedagogy in the COVID-19 Pandemic in Italy* by Francesca Costa and Olivia Mair, not coincidentally the final one in the book since it deals with a recent topic, represents the new reality of EMI teaching that has arisen during COVID-19. The chapter explores online input in EMI in the COVID era through a questionnaire sent to 73 teachers and the analysis of video-recordings, followed by two stimulated recall sections to elicit from teachers the online input strategies implemented during this period and uncover any differences between their teaching methods before, during and after the COVID-19 pandemic and between online teaching through the L1 or L2.

Precisely because of the diversity of contexts and methodologies, this book is particularly suitable for inclusion in this series. Moreover, because this series (edited by Annette Bradford and Howard Brown) is also practical in nature, each contribution will try to outline the real implications and repercussions for EMI teaching.

Note

1 Piske, T., & Young-Scholten, M. (2008). *Input matters in SLA*. Multilingual Matters.

References

Aguilar, M. (2017). Engineering lecturers' views on CLIL and EMI. *International Journal of Bilingual Education and Bilingualism*, 20(6), 722–735. https://doi.org/10.1080/1367005 0.2015.1073664

Airey, J. (2011). Talking about teaching in English: Swedish university lecturers' experiences of changing teaching language. *Ibérica*, 22, 35–54.

Basturkmen, H., & Shackleford, N. (2015). How content lecturers help students with language: An observational study of language-related episodes in interaction in first year accounting classrooms. *English for Specific Purposes*, 37(1), 87–97.

Block, D., & Khan, S. (Eds.). (2021). *The secret life of English-medium instruction in higher education: Examining microphenomena in context*. Routledge.

Bowles, H., & Murphy, A. (Eds.). (2020). *English-medium instruction and the internationalisation of universities*. Palgrave Macmillan.

Brown, H., & Bradford, A. (2016). EMI, CLIL, & CBI: Differing approaches and goals. In P. Clements, A. Krause, & H. Brown (Eds.), *Transformation in language education* (pp. 328–334). JALT.

Carroll, S. (2001). *Input and evidence: The raw material of second language acquisition*. John Benjamins Publishing Group.

Coonan, C. M. (2002). *La lingua straniera veicolare*. UTET.

Costa, F. (2012). Focus on form in ICLHE lectures. *AILAReview*, 25, 30–47.

Costa, F. (2016). *CLIL (Content and language integrated learning) through English in Italian higher education*. LED.
Costa, F. (2017). Defamiliarisation vs automatism: The cognitive added value of CL(English)IL – humour and other strategies. In C. M. Coonan, L. Favaro, & M. Menegale (Eds.), *A journey through the content and language integrated learning landscape* (pp. 123–139). Cambridge Scholars Publishing.
Costa, F., & Mair, O. (2022). Multimodality and pronunciation in ICLHE (integrating content and language in higher education) training. *Innovation in Language Learning and Teaching*. doi:10.1080/17501229.2022.2053130
Costa, F., & Mariotti, C. (2021). Strategies to enhance comprehension in EMI lectures: Examples from the Italian context. In A. Doiz & D. Lasagabaster (Eds.), *Global perspectives on language aspects and teacher development in English-medium instruction* (pp. 80–99). Routledge.
Dafouz Milne, E., & Núñez Perucha, B. (2010). Metadiscursive devices in university lectures. A contrastive analysis of L1 and L2 teacher performance. In C. Dalton Puffer, T. Nikula, & U. Smit (Eds.), *Language use and language learning in CLIL classrooms* (pp. 213–232). AILA Applied Linguistics Series, 7.
Dafouz Milne, E., Nuñez Perucha, B., & Sancho, C. (2007). Analysing stance in a CLIL university context: Non-native speaker use of personal pronouns and modal verbs. *The International Journal of Bilingual Education and Bilingualism, 10*(5), 647–662.
Dafouz Milne, E., & Smit, U. (2020). *ROAD-MAPPING English medium education in the internationalised university*. Palgrave Macmillan.
Dimova, S., Hultren, K., & Jensen, C. (2015). *English-medium instruction in European higher education*. De Gruyter Mouton.
Doiz, A., Lasagabaster, D., & Sierra, J. M. (2013). Future challenges for English-medium instruction at the tertiary level. In A. Doiz, D. Lasagabaster, & J. M. Sierra (Eds.), *English-medium instruction at universities* (pp. 213–221). Multilingual Matters.
Echevarría, J., Vogt, M. E., & Short, D. (2008). *Making content comprehensible for English language learners: The SIOP model*. Allyn & Bacon.
Ellis, R. (2012). *The study of second language acquisition*. Oxford University Press.
Gass, S. M., & Madden, C. G. (1985). *Input in second language acquisition*. Newbury House.
Hong, J., & Basturkmen, H. (2020). Incidental attention to academic language during content teaching in two EMI classes in South Korean high schools. *Journal of English for Academic Purposes, 48*. https://doi.org/10.1016/j.jeap.2020.100921
Hulstijn, J. H. (2003). Incidental and intentional learning. In C. J. Doughty & M. H. Long (Eds.), *The handbook of second language learning* (pp. 349–381). Blackwell Publishing.
Jenkins, J., & Mauranen, A. (Eds.). (2019). *Linguistic diversity on the EMI campus*. Routledge.
Kasper, L. F. (2000). *Content-based ESL instruction*. Lawrence Erlbaum Associates.
Krashen, S. (1982). *Principles and practice in second language acquisition*. Pergamon.

Krashen, S. (1993). *The power of reading*. Libraries Unlimited.
Lasagabaster, D. (2022). *English-medium instruction in higher education*. Cambridge University Press.
Long, M. (1996). The role of the linguistic environment in second language acquisition. In W. C. Ritchie & T. K. Bhatia (Eds.), *Handbook of second language acquisition* (pp. 413–468). Academic Press.
Long, M. H., & Robinson, P. (1998). Focus on form. Theory, research and practice. In C. Doughty & J. Williams (Eds.), *Focus on form in classroom second language acquisition* (pp. 15–41). Cambridge University Press.
Macaro, E. (2018). *English medium instruction*. Oxford University Press.
Macaro, E. (2019). Exploring the role of language in English medium instruction. *International Journal of Bilingual Education and Bilingualism*, *23*(3), 263–276.
Mariotti, C. (2007). *Interaction strategies in English-medium instruction*. Franco Angeli.
Mariotti, C. (2016). Strategie di presentazione dell'input in contesti CLIL. In A. Valentini (Ed.), *L'input per l'acquisizione di lingue seconde: Strutturazione, percezione, elaborazione* (pp. 101–116). Cesati.
McKinley, J., & Galloway, N. (Eds.). (2022). *English-medium instruction practices in higher education: International perspectives*. Bloomsbury.
Mohan, B. (1986). *Language and content*. Addison-Wesley Publishing Company.
Molino, A. (2015). Comprensione e interazione nelle lezioni universitarie in lingua inglese. *RiCognizioni*, *2*(4), 129–143.
Molino, A. (2017). Repetition and rephrasing in physical sciences and engineering English-medium lectures in Italy. In C. Boggio & A. Molino (Eds.), *English in Italy: Linguistic, educational and professional challenges* (pp. 182–202). FrancoAngeli.
Molino, A. (2018). 'What I'm speaking is almost English . . .': A corpus-based study of metadiscourse in English-medium lectures at an Italian university. *Educational Sciences: Theory and Practice*, *18*(4), 935–956.
Molino, A., Dimova, S., Kling, J., & Larsen, S. (2022). *The evolution of EMI research in European higher education*. Routledge.
Morell, T. (2020). EMI teacher training with a multimodal and interactive approach: A new horizon for LSP specialists. *Language Value*, *12*(1), 56–87.
Paulsrud, B. A., Tian, Z., & Toth, J. (Eds.). (2021). *English-medium instruction and translanguaging*. Multilingual Matters.
Pecorari, D. (2020). English medium instruction: Disintegrating language and content. In D. Slobodanka & J. Kling (Eds.), *Integrating content and language in multilingual universities* (pp. 15–36). Springer.
Piske, T., & Young-Scholten, M. (2008). *Input matters in SLA*. Multilingual Matters.
Richards, J., & Pun, J. (2022). *Teaching and learning in English medium instruction*. Routledge.
Roquet, H., Vraciu, A., Nicolás-Conesa, F., & Pérez-Vidal, C. (2020). Adjunct instruction in higher education: Examining the effects on English foreign language

proficiency. *International Journal of Bilingual Education and Bilingualism*. doi:10.1080/13670050.2020.1765967

Sah, P. R. (2022). A research agenda for English-medium instruction. Conversations with scholars at the research fronts. *Journal of English-Medium Instruction, 1*(1), 124–136.

Sharwood Smith, M. (1986). Comprehension versus acquisition: Two ways of processing input. *Applied Linguistics, 7*(3), 239–256.

Stohler, U. (2006). The acquisition of knowledge in bilingual learning: An empirical study of the role of language in content learning. *Vienna English Working Papers, 3*(06), 41–46.

Valentini, A., & Grassi, R. (2017). Descrivere il processo: l'input, l'innesco dell'acquisizione. In C. Andorno, A. Valentini, & R. Grassi (Eds.), *Verso una nuova lingua. Capire l'acquisizione di L2* (pp. 89–120). UTET.

VanPatten, B. (2009). Processing matters in input enhancement. In T. Piske & M. Young-Scholten (Eds.), *Input matters in SLA* (pp. 47–61). Multilingual Matters.

Vraciu, A., & Curell, H. (2022). Language learning opportunities in native vs. nonnative EMI lecturer input: Insights for a language-aware approach to EMI teacher training. *Innovation in Language Learning and Teaching*. doi:10.1080/17501229.2022.2059666

Wächter, B., & Maiworm, F. (Eds.). (2014). *English-taught programmes in European higher education. The state of play in 2014*. ACA Papers on International Cooperation in Education. Lemmens.

Wilkinson, R. (2009). Inequity in teaching content in different languages: A case study of an English native speaker teaching professional skills in Dutch. In D. Veronesi & C. Nickenig (Eds.), *Bi- and multilingual universities: European perspectives and beyond* (pp. 307–316). Bozen-Bolzano University Press.

Wode, H. (1999). Incidental vocabulary acquisition in the foreign language classroom. *Studies in Second Language Acquisition, 21*(2), 243–258.

2 Analysing Classroom Discourse and the Role of Productive Thinking in Teacher–Student Exchanges

Aintzane Doiz and David Lasagabaster

Introduction

Teachers raise questions to guide meaning-making interactions and to scaffold their students' learning. Teacher questions are also important because they affect the nature of students' thinking and reasoning while determining the quality and the level of students' participation. That is, they can become indices of quality teaching. For all these reasons, the role of questioning exchanges is well worth exploring (Chin, 2007).

However, little (e.g. Dafouz & Garcia, 2013) has been carried out regarding its impact on English-Medium Instruction (EMI) at university, the context for the present investigation. Our study aims to help fill the gap by analysing teacher-led questions at the University of the Basque Country UPV/EHU in Spain and to identify how EMI teachers of history use questions and what type of questions they fall back on.

The Role of Questions in Classroom Discourse and Their Analysis in the Present Study

In this study, we considered the following three aspects which could be germane to describe EMI teachers' use of questions in classrooms in our study. The first one deals with the consideration of the classification of questions into closed and open. The former encompasses questions that only require one word or constituent to be answered appropriately (yes/no questions and closed-led wh-questions). Open questions, conversely, require students to convey a thought or statement in their own non-predetermined words. They include questions about facts, opinions or explanations that cannot be answered with one word or constituent.

Secondly, we considered the distinction between authoritative and dialogic classroom discourse (Chin, 2007; Scott et al., 2006). In the case of

DOI: 10.4324/9781003258407-2

authoritative (or more traditional) discourse, the teacher conveys knowledge and the expected responses to the questions posed are typically single words. Most authoritative exchanges seek to evaluate students' knowledge through closed questions that require a predetermined and low-order, cognitive-level short response. The teacher acknowledges right answers and corrects the wrong ones. Conversely, in dialogic discourse (or under a constructivist approach), the teacher invites students to explore and debate different points of view. Its aim is to foster students' debate about previous contributions through open questions with no content boundaries. This entails that answers are longer and involve high-order cognitive levels. In dialogic questions, the teacher assumes a neutral stance (in contrast with the evaluative position in authoritative questions) and usually avoids evaluative comments while seeking clarifications.

In the third place, we used Chin's (2007) framework because it allows us to identify the questions which promote productive thinking among the students, one of the objectives of the present study. Productive thinking accounts for the interconnection of concepts into a conceptual framework as opposed to their presentation of isolated facts and the encouragement of the role of students as active recipients of knowledge while advancing students' thinking. Chin identified 4 main approaches and 11 specific questioning strategies in the use of teacher-led questions to stimulate productive thinking among the students. The first broad approach is *Socratic questioning*, which "uses a series of questions to prompt and guide student thinking" and is used to encourage students' generation of ideas from previous knowledge and reasoning. It includes the use of pumping, reflective toss and constructive challenge. The second strategy is *verbal jigsaw*, whose main goal is to focus on "the use of scientific terminology, keywords and phrases to form integrated propositional statements" and strengthen the students' language skills. It involves the use of association of keywords and phrases, and verbal cloze. The third category, *semantic tapestry*, is used to establish conceptual relationships among diverse ideas "into a conceptual framework", usually through the strategies of multi-pronged questioning and stimulating multi-modal thinking. The fourth and final approach, *framing*, introduces a topic, problem or issues through questions and can be found in question-based preludes, question-based outlines and question-based summary (Chin, 2007, p. 823).

While the role of questions in previous EMI research is scant, studies conclude that questions foster students' reasoning and comprehension of subject matter. For example, Suviniitty (2010), after asking EMI students, concluded that lectures with a higher degree of interaction and questions were easier to understand. Sánchez-García (2020) explored teachers' practices in Spanish and EMI lectures, the number of questions being largely similar in both contexts. However, there were almost twice as many managerial questions (related to classroom management and organisation) in EMI lectures, which revealed lecturers' concern about students' understanding of lecture organisation in the latter. Finally, Chang (2012) investigated whether disciplinary cultures influenced the patterns of questions in different disciplines. The results showed "far more similarities than differences between the soft and hard fields" (p. 112), the influence of genre (the lecture as a genre) outweighing that of disciplinary culture.

With all this in mind, our study is aimed at analysing teacher-fronted questioning during whole-class discussions. In particular, in this study, we entertain the following two research questions:

RQ1: What is the teacher/student class interaction like? (analysed via closed/open questions and authoritative/dialogic discourse)
RQ2: Does the questioning approach used by the teachers promote productive thinking? (Chin's framework)

The Study

For the present study, we observed and videotaped eight two-hour sessions offered by four male history teachers at the University of the Basque Country UPV/EHU in Spain. These were small classes (fewer than 25 students) that were chosen because in mass lectures teachers' authoritative talk tends to dominate and there is usually little room for questions. Once the classes were transcribed verbatim by a research assistant, we selected all the verbal interactions which contained a teacher-led question. The corpus was made up of a total of 65,430 words: Teacher 1 (T1) produced 17,661 words; Teacher 2 (T2), 17,307; Teacher 3 (T3), 14,595 and Teacher 4 (T4), 15,867.

The four participants were highly experienced teachers with experience ranging from 16 to 25 years, although their involvement in EMI courses was more limited ranging from 2 to 7 years. All the teachers had an equivalent of the C1 level of the Common European Framework of Reference for Languages, a prerequisite to be allowed to teach content classes in English.

Method

In order to address research question 1, we adopted a quantitative approach of the data. With the help of the video-recordings, a research assistant first identified the teacher-led questions in the transcripts by marking the utterances whose intonation pattern and/or syntactic pattern were that of a question (Chin, 2007). These were cross-checked by the two authors of the paper. The authors decided to discard the questions that were replicas and repetitions with minor changes to a previous question. Then we classified the questions into three categories, namely, self-answered questions (responded to by the teachers themselves), unanswered questions (those without a reply) and questions addressed by the students. Questions were further categorised into closed and open to determine whether the teacher–student exchanges were predominately authoritative or dialogic.

Since the teachers differed in the total number of words they uttered in their lessons, we followed Zhang and Lo's practice (2021) to normalise the data per 1,000 words in order to make the data comparable. Thus, in addition to stating the tokens of questions posited, we provided their percentage per 1,000 words in the results section.

Research question 2 was approached qualitatively and was drawn from Chin's framework (2007). We first identified the episodes that prompted "deeper thinking or move thinking forward" (Chin, 2007, p. 822). Then, we selected representative instances of the four broad questioning approaches posited by Chin and several of her specific questioning strategies as a means to illustrate the role of questions to promote productive thinking.

Results

We present the results for research question 1 and research question 2 next.

What Is the Teacher/Student Interaction Like?

A total of 372 questions were recorded (Table 2.1), fewer than half of which (169, 45.4%) were actually answered by the students. The rest of the questions either were addressed by the teachers themselves (128, 34.4%) or did not receive any reply (75, 20.2%). In addition, certain personal traits were noted among the teachers. In particular, the teachers greatly differed with respect to the amount and the frequency of the questions they asked, with T1, T2 and T3 posing questions more than twice as frequently (8.66‰, 5.5‰ and 5.48‰, respectively) as T4 (2.71‰). The teachers also undertook different questioning practices because T2 produced a significantly higher number of self-answered questions than the other teachers (3.17‰), while T1 had the highest rate of unanswered (2.09‰) and answered questions (4.64‰).

When the focus is placed on the questions that were actually answered by the students (n=169), we noted that the majority were closed (94), although there was also a significant number of open questions posed (75), as shown in Table 2.2. Since closed questions tend to be associated with the authoritative approach, while open questions with the dialogic approach, it appears

Analysing Classroom Discourse and Productive Thinking   17

Table 2.1 An overview of the teacher-led questions normalised at 1,000 words

	T1 Tokens/‰	T2 Tokens/‰	T3 Tokens/‰	T4 Tokens/‰	Total
Self-answered questions by the teachers	34/1.96	55/3.17	25/1.71	14/0.88	**128**
Unanswered questions	37/2.09	7/0.40	26/1.78	5/0.31	**75**
Questions answered by the students	82/4.64	34/1.96	29/1.98	24/1.51	**169**
Total	**153/8.66**	**96/5.5**	**80/5.48**	**43/2.71**	372

Table 2.2 Closed questions versus open questions

	Closed questions		Open questions		
	Yes/no	Wh-word	Why	Wh-word	Opinion/Evaluation What do you think?
Answered by the students	36	58	18	44	13
Total 169		**94**		**75**	

that, although the authoritative approach predominated in the interactions, the dialogic approach had a considerable presence as well.

As can be seen from Table 2.2, most of the closed and open questions were wh-questions. We detected a high number of "why" questions among the open questions (18 out of 75), which is the reason why we included them in a column of their own. The use of "why" questions in tertiary education is very important, as these questions enable students to ascribe the causes and reasons for events, make personal judgements and take an ideological stance. Extract 1 illustrates a typical dialogic teacher/student interaction episode in which the open questions were designed to ask the students' opinion ("do you think that . . . ?"), to elaborate their thoughts ("why do you say that?") and to engage the students by rephrasing the question ("So from the global point of view do you think that . . . ?"). These questions are cognitively demanding and promote critical thinking.

Extract 1:

> T1: do you think that our dependence on fossil fuels has really ended with the threat of Malthusianism crisis?
> T1: what do you think Unai *(name of a student)*?

S: I think that's false because for example eh in the Dutch republic the population is xxx and the main countries xxx.
T1: but that was in Dutch republic, right, now?
S: no.
T1: now Holland is not a republic, it is a kingdom.
S: yes Holland xxx.
T1: why do you say so?
S: well the region of Holland is quite high and xxx.
T1: yeah but but Holland has been importing from at least the 15th century its goods. So from the global point of view do you think that the earth to put this in that way do you think that the earth can say well Malthusianism disappeared once and for all thanks to the industrial revolution # and thanks especially to the use of fossil fuels? Because this is part of the most interesting debates in our time.

Open questions and closed questions were often found in the same teacher/student episode and followed a pattern according to which open questions were frequently replaced by more specific questions and by closed questions. This phenomenon referred to as *reformulation* was also observed by Sánchez-García (2020) in an EMI classroom at a Spanish University. Extract 2 is a good illustration of reformulation, in which T1 replaced the open question "What does this mean? Smithian model of economic growth?" by the more specific questions of "You know who was Adam Smith?", "Who was Adam Smith?", and the closed question "What was the title of the book?" Hence, the first open question that was conducive to a dialogic/constructivist dialogue was replaced by more specific or closed questions associated with a more traditional discourse.

Extract 2:

T1: Well, what is this, eeeh, this expression? *(writing on the board).* What does Smithian model of economic growth mean?
T1: You know who was Adam Smith? This goes specifically for those students of economics in this room. So, who was Adam Smith? . . .
S: The father of the modern economy.
T: Not of the modern economy the modern economic theory. . . . there's a difference between economy and economics. So, Adam Smith was the founder of the modern economic theory or the modern economics. . . .
T1: And what was the title of book? This is very important.

In summary, the data revealed that class interactions were characterised by a significant amount of questions which did not elicit any response from the students (e.g. self-answered and unanswered questions). It may be the case that the teachers answered questions themselves as a means of taking pressure off the students, as the latter might find articulating complex ideas in English quite challenging. Unanswered open questions appear to have been used to introduce a new topic or to emphasise the importance of a specific point in some contexts, and therefore no student response was really required. However, the role of these questions needs to be investigated in more detail.

In addition, we saw that teacher individual traits permeated the class interactions, in terms of the number of questions asked and the questions answered by the students. For instance, T1, T2 and T3 relied on the use of questions more frequently than T4, T2's interactions were characterised by the use of self-answered questions, and only T1 had some success in getting students to respond to his questions. By looking at the kinds of questions that students responded to, we were also able to conclude that the authoritative approach was more prevalent than the dialogic approach, but the dichotomy between these two approaches was not clear-cut in all instances, as sometimes teachers adopted the two approaches in the same episode. Finally, while the reformulation of questions may have been used to encourage student participation, yet, it may actually prevent the students from engaging in discourse and "end up narrowing down their opportunities to interact" (Sánchez-García, 2020, p. 46).

Does the Questioning Approach Used by the Teachers Promote Productive Thinking?

Our analysis of the classroom interactions revealed that the teachers indeed used the four broad approaches of Socratic questioning, verbal jigsaw, semantic tapestry and framing put forward by Chin (2007), thereby promoting productive thinking among the students. However, since more than half of the questions were answered by the teachers themselves or were not answered by the students as concluded in the analysis of RQ1, it appears that the students did not participate in the process of productive thinking so actively. In addition, since our goal was not to state whether one strategy was favoured over the others by the teachers, we did not quantify them. In this section, we will be illustrating the four questioning approaches and, due to space constraints, only some of the specific strategies undertaken by the teachers.

Extract 3 illustrates *Socratic questioning* in which the teacher asks a series of questions with the aim to promote students' thinking as opposed to giving the information to the students straight away. In this particular extract, T3 wanted the students to reflect on the importance of Italy for the kingdoms of France and Castile-Aragon in Spain during medieval times. The students made a few proposals which were not what the teacher really wanted to get at (e.g. Italy was important because of the Pope, because it had a commercial hub, its fleets and its commercial routes). Instead of providing the right answer to the question himself, T3 used the *pumping* strategy associated with *Socratic questioning* by encouraging students to give more information and to "further articulate their thoughts and ideas" through explicit requests (e.g. "What more?", "Apart from . . . ?") and positive feedback (e.g. "very well", "yes") (Chin, 2007, p. 824). He also repeated the student's answer before posing another question frequently (e.g. "Commercial hub, okay? Not only in the Mediterranean Sea but . . .. What more?"). This is a common practice also observed by Chin in her data (2007, p. 825) which serves to encourage student participation.

Extract 3:

T3: Well, why was Italy so important for Castile-Aragon and for France? . . .
S: Because the Pope eh xxx.
T3: the Pope very well mm? The religious power was in the middle of the centre of Italy.
T3: What more? What happened at this time with eh Italy? Italy's the principal?
S: Commercial hub.
T3: Commercial hub, okay? Not only in the Mediterranean Sea but also in all Europe. What more? Apart from being the principal commercial centre?
T3: It was also? Why was (*it*) the principal commercial centre in Europe? Thanks to what?
S: The fleet? And the fleets they had.
T3: Yes. But apart from this?
S: Commercial routes.
T3: From the east very well but apart from this? What they commercialised from Italy? Which was the stronger item in Italy?
T3: The? Textiles okay?

Extract 4 instantiates the *verbal jigsaw* approach in which the specialised terminology and keywords are the focus of the teacher/student interaction. In particular, the specific strategy of *verbal cloze* was used in which the teacher paused in the middle of a question to give the students the opportunity to provide the missing specialised word which is part of "a network of related concepts" (Chin, 2007, p. 826). In this extract, T1 wanted the students to talk about the concept of "division of labour" as an essential element in the phenomenon of Adam Smith's theory of economic growth.

Extract 4:

T1: Nevertheless, one could wonder at the end of the day, how these, how did these economies eeh grow? What's the way of achieving economic growth? Where, where we can find the causes of economic growth?
T1: And this is why I told you to read Adam's Smith books
T1: What Adam Smith trying to communicate? Because in these, in these chapters Adam Smith is addressing the basic question of economic growth and, according to Adam Smith economic growth rest, rests basically on?
S: The division of labour. It's said that the division of labour is better than to work in to make something xxx.
T1: By your own.
S: By your own.

Extract 5 contains a case of *semantic tapestry* in which T2 used the strategy of *stimulating multimodal thinking* as a means to "building conceptual and relational understanding in students" (Chin, 2007, p. 829). In this particular episode, the teacher began his lesson by talking about the invention of several new devices (e.g. the astrolabe, the compass and the lateen sail) that facilitated the exploration of the seas and were crucial to the discovery of new territories between the fourteenth and sixteenth centuries. He did this with the help of the Internet and a Ted talk. Then he emphasised the idea that, as a result of these discoveries, a more accurate knowledge of the world ensued. To help students arrive at this conclusion by themselves, he used a different mode, the visual mode. In particular, T2 made the students reflect on the development of the geographical knowledge of the world next by means of maps drawn in different historical periods. By guiding the students with his questions, they were able to establish relationships between what they could see on the maps and the new geographical knowledge at different historical periods, encouraging visual thinking in the process.

Extract 5:

T2: Well was the image of the earth as it was described by Ptolemy? Yes or no?
S: Not exactly.
T2: Why not?
S: Because the island of the land. Ptolemy was wrong.
T2: Have you noticed this strange patch of land here?
S: Yes.
T2: What is this?

S: Scandinavia.
T2: Scandinavia. And that one?
S: This is the island xxx
T2: Iceland. Scandinavia. . . . And why? Why did they put # those lands over there # in such extension?
S: Because Ptolemy didn't know that xxx islands
T2: Yeah that's true.

Multimodal thinking was also encouraged by the teachers through the use of other multimodal resources such as songs (T2), texts written in old Spanish (T3), paintings (T3), references to movies (T1) and documentaries (T4). Hence, this is a strategy that was frequently exploited by the teachers probably as a means to make their classes more attractive.

Extract 6 illustrates *framing*, another approach that stimulates productive thinking, by means of the teaching strategy of *question-based prelude* (Chin, 2007). This strategy is used to introduce a new topic and to organise the discourse "instead of just plain teaching-telling" (p. 833). It tends to include questions answered by the teachers themselves, making the process of "the teacher's thinking visible" (p. 833). In this extract, T1 introduced the new topic of the rise of the British Empire as a world economic power and the reasons that were responsible for it with the question "Is Britain well-endowed with natural resources during the early modern period?" The question served to contextualise the topic he wanted to talk about and, instead of letting the students answer the question, he answered it immediately with a short answer ("not really") first, and then with a long answer. Next, he posed the key question "Why (did everything change on the eve of the industrial revolution)?" This question and its short answer announced the content of that day's lesson ("And this is what we are going to see in this part of the lesson") and are part of the *question-based prelude* strategy. In this teacher-led episode, T1 exposed his train of thought, guided the students with his questions and answers to follow and helped them develop their own thinking processes at the same time.

Extract 6:

T1: Is Britain well endowed with natural resources during the early modern period? Not really. It has got coal, but coal is not important from an economic point of view before industrial revolution, and in fact, at the beginning of the early modern period, England is a small country not very important and it's considered in the group of the most backward and less developed European economies around the year, eeeeeh, 1500.

T1: When compared to France or the Italian republics, England is a poor country, is basically a poor country, the second rank, a second class country, something like that. However, on the eve of the industrial revolution everything changed. Why?
T1: Because if there was a country who achieved success in its mercantile policies, it was probably Britain. Everybody followed the same policies but Britain was the most successful country in this effort, okay?
T1: And this is what we are going to see in this part of the lesson.

In sum, the teachers tried to foster and develop productive thinking in the students through the use of specific strategies within the four broad approaches to questioning posited by Chin (2007). However, since the students tended not to participate actively in the classes, the questions posed by the teachers were frequently answered by the teachers themselves or were left unanswered, perhaps limiting to some extent the presence of rich interactions. When the students did answer the teacher-led questions, their replies were not always as elaborated as the teachers might have hoped for. Nevertheless, we may conclude from the analysis of the data that the questions asked by the teachers were clearly geared to stimulate productive thinking in the students.

Conclusions

Our analysis of the teacher/student interactions has shown that both the authoritative approach and the dialogic approach had considerable presence in this EMI context. We have also seen that the teachers tried to foster students' productive thinking through the use of the four approaches to ask questions and their specific strategies identified by Chin (2007). These strategies tried to make students justify and elaborate their ideas. However, our data revealed that the use of these strategies tended to trigger meagre answers from the students. In fact, the teacher/student exchanges were frequently limited to one question and one student answer. A possible reason for the students' scarce participation may be the Spanish tertiary education, students' unwillingness to actively participate in lectures in general and the difficulties posed by their limited English proficiency. The teachers may also have a bearing on this issue as many of the questions they posed were answered by the teachers themselves.

We believe our study has significant implications for EMI teacher training. Since EMI students themselves believe that the comprehensibility of lectures improves with increased question-led interaction (Suviniitty, 2010), a pedagogical implication to be drawn from our data would be to encourage EMI teachers to think about how they use questions in class, with the expectation that they will employ more constructivist practices in their teaching. In line with the work by Sedova (2017), observing excerpts from their video-recorded classes could be a very practical way to foster reflection on what impact their questions have on students' participation. Furthermore, discussion of video-recorded classes with the teachers may also encourage a reflection on the teachers' reformulation of open-to-closed questions and the role that self-answered and unanswered questions play in their classes.

Acknowledgements

This work was supported by the Spanish Ministry of Science and Innovation [grant number PID2020-117882GB-I00] and the Basque Government [grant number IT1426-22].

Appendix 1. Coding Conventions

T1, T2, T3, T4 = Teacher 1, Teacher 2, Teacher 3, Teacher 4
S = student
xxx = inaudible utterances
(*italics*) = words added to make the utterances comprehensible
[. . .] = some words were deleted that were irrelevant to the discussion

References

Chang, Y.-Y. (2012). The use of questions by professors in lectures given in English: Influences of disciplinary cultures. *English for Specific Purposes*, *31*(2), 103–116.

Chin, C. (2007). Teacher questioning in science classrooms: Approaches that stimulate productive thinking. *Journal of Research in Science Teaching*, *44*(6), 815–843.

Dafouz, E., & Garcia, D. S. (2013). 'Does everybody understand?' Teacher questions across disciplines in English-mediated university lectures: An exploratory study. *Language Value*, *5*(1), 129–151.

Sánchez-García, D. (2020). Mapping lecture questions and their pedagogical goals in Spanish- and English-medium instruction. *Journal of Immersion and Content-Based Language Education*, *8*(1), 28–52.

Scott, P. H., Mortimer, E. F., & Aguiar, O. G. (2006). The tension between authoritative and dialogic discourse: A fundamental characteristic of meaning making interactions in high school science lessons. *Science Education*, *90*(4), 605–631.

Sedova, K. (2017). A case study of a transition to dialogic teaching as a process of gradual change. *Teaching and Teacher Education*, *67*, 278–290.

Suviniitty, J. (2010). Lecturers' questions and student perception of lecture comprehension. *Helsinki English Studies*, *6*, 44–57.

Zhang, L., & Lo, Y. Y. (2021). EMI teachers' use of interactive metadiscourse in lecture organization and knowledge construction. In D. Lasagabaster & A. Doiz (Eds.), *Language use in English-medium instruction at university: International perspectives on teacher practice* (pp. 56–79). Routledge.

3 Development and Application of the *Framework for the Analysis of Vocabulary Language-Related Episodes*

Helen Basturkmen and Jiye Hong

Introduction

An emerging thrust of English-Medium Instruction research examines what occurs within EMI classrooms (Sahan, 2021). The present chapter aims to develop the understanding of what occurs within EMI classes with an inquiry into incidental attention to vocabulary in disciplinary classroom interaction.

It is generally understood that novices to a discipline acquire a good deal of vocabulary through incidental exposure to words in reading materials and classroom interaction as well as through any planned vocabulary teaching interventions that may be available. Recent research indicates that episodes concerning language issues occur with some regularity in content classroom interaction and that such episodes often address vocabulary. See studies in EMI in Spain (Doiz & Lasagabaster, 2021), Italy (Costa, 2012), New Zealand (Basturkmen & Shackleford, 2015; McLaughlin & Parkinson, 2018), Brazil (Martinez et al., 2021) and South Korea (Hong, 2021a, 2021b; Hong & Basturkmen, 2020).

The chapter has two main aims. Firstly, it presents the development of a framework for analysing vocabulary-focused episodes that arise incidentally in EMI classroom interaction. Secondly, it illustrates an application of this framework in a new analysis of 180 language-related episodes collected in prior research in Mathematics and Accounting classes in a South Korean university context (Hong, 2021b).

Research Questions

The analysis focused on three research questions:

1) What proportion of vocabulary LREs address meaning, form and lexical choice?

2) To what extent do meaning and form-focused LREs target single-word units compared to formulaic sequences?
3) What proportion of lexical choice LREs focus on alternative or preferred lexical choices?

Language-Related Episodes (LREs)

The term Language_Related Episode (LRE) from the Second Language Acquisition (SLA) literature refers to any part of a dialogue where participants "talk about the language they are producing, question their language use or correct themselves or others" (Swain & Lapkin, 1998, p. 326). In disciplinary teaching, LREs, or incidental time-outs from the primary discussion of conceptual content to focus on language, provide important opportunities for lecturers and teachers to draw students' attention to the vocabulary of the discipline's register or to correct their students' use or understanding of this vocabulary, and for students to notice disciplinary uses of vocabulary or check their understanding of it. Examples 1 and 2 illustrate vocabulary LREs in Accounting class interaction. In Example 1, the Lecturer uses the term "creditors" and quickly follows this with an explanation of what the term means. In Example 2, a student checks whether "net earnings", a term that the lecturer had just used, is the same as "net income".

Example 1. LRE targeting "creditors"

LECTURER: You may need to borrow money from one side. You need to borrow money from creditors, those people you borrow money from like a bank, a commercial company.

Example 2. LREs targeting "net earnings" and "net income"

STUDENT: Are net earnings net income?
LECTURER: Yes, yes, you can call it net income. What's that? What's the meaning of net income again? It's the final amount of money after you minus all the expenses from sales, right?

Vocabulary-focused LREs are generally subtle and transient elements of disciplinary class interaction. Research suggests that they arise because of perceived or anticipated student difficulties with vocabulary and that they serve as means by which lecturers can briefly address vocabulary issues within content teaching (Basturkmen & Shackleford, 2015; Hong & Basturkmen, 2020). To date, information about vocabulary LREs has generally been limited to rate or frequency counts, that is, counts of the number of LREs that address vocabulary. A framework and approach that would enable teachers, lecturers and researchers to examine vocabulary LREs in detail have been missing. This led to the present study, which aimed to scrutinise vocabulary LREs to build more detailed understanding of the kinds of lexical knowledge and types of words they address. The work led to the development of the *Framework for the Analysis of Vocabulary LREs*.

Incidental Vocabulary Acquisition

Incidental vocabulary acquisition is the picking up of new words while learners are engaged in using the language during reading, listening, speaking or writing when there is no planned or prior intention to learn new words (Rot, 2013). Lack of prior intention to learn does not preclude the possibility that learners will direct their attention to processing words during skills activities (Hulstijin, 2001). It is generally recognised that learners cannot develop a lexicon entirely through deliberate learning, such as through memorising words lists. Learning new words entails learning the functional and syntactic aspects of the words as well as their meanings and forms. (Nation, 2001; Rot, 2013).

Ellis (1994) argued that reading is an ideal means for incidental vocabulary acquisition as printed language provides time for learners to process new words. However, research findings indicated that relatively few words are picked up during reading (Horst et al., 1998; Rot, 2013), although recent investigation indicates that earlier research may have underestimated the extent (Rot, 2013). Reading does not necessarily induce the kind of noticing of new word forms or new meanings for familiar forms that enables form-meaning connections to become stored in the memory. Rot (2013) suggests that processing a reading text for comprehension and processing it to commit words to memory may involve conflicting cognitive processes. L2 readers may be able to grasp the meaning of a text without needing to notice new word forms appearing in the text and although they may notice new word forms, they may not be able to infer the meaning conveyed either because the text does not provide sufficient contextual clues or because the reader does not have the requisite background knowledge to infer the meaning (Rot, 2013).

Classroom interaction provides a potentially important site for incidental vocabulary acquisition. The lecturer is present in real time in the classroom interaction and can deal with vocabulary-related questions and difficulties as they arise and can make spur-of-the-moment decisions about when and if to highlight vocabulary. Lecturers may prompt learners to notice new word forms and are available if students cannot infer the meaning of the words used. Prior research into LREs in EMI has largely been limited to comparing the relative frequency of episodes that focus on vocabulary compared to other linguistic targets, such as grammar (Doiz & Lasagabaster, 2021; Hong, 2021b), the teaching strategy involved (Doiz & Lasagabaster, 2021) and students' appreciation of such LREs (Martinez et al., 2021) but not the precise nature of the lexical information targeted.

Formulaic Sequences

Collocations represent tendencies for words to co-occur and are one type of formulaic sequence. The term formulaic sequence can be defined as any holistic multi-word entity, including entities that are semantically transparent (Wray, 2021). Examples of collocations, or formulaic sequences, in Accounting include "residual value" and "accounts payable". Eye movement and brain electrical activity tracking reading research suggest that formulaic sequences are produced and processed holistically (Wray, 2021). Recent corpus analytical research has identified collocations in academic speaking compared to academic writing (Simpson-Vlach & Ellis, 2010) and collocations in specific disciplines (Green & Lambert, 2018).

Acquisition of formulaic language is important for disciplinary novices who need to acquire the discipline's linguistic register. Formulaic language provides advantages in processing and understanding texts and in being judged as proficient and fluent language users (Coxhead, 2018). Formulaic sequences can act as markers belonging to the group that uses the language (Coxhead, 2018; Wray, 2021). Using formulaic language enables learners to produce complete ideas with relatively limited effort and to express ideas as others would, thus making it likely that the messages they wish to express are correctly interpreted (Wray, 2021). The present study examined the extent LREs targeted single- and multi-word units, or collocations. As the study was based in EMI settings (Accounting and Mathematics classrooms), the collocations examined were largely formulaic sequences of disciplinary language use.

The remainder of the chapter is organised into three parts. Firstly, it presents the *Framework* and describes the approach by which it was developed. Secondly, the chapter illustrates an application of the *Framework* in a frequency analysis. The final part of the chapter provides suggestions for ways researchers and teachers might apply the *Framework* in their endeavours to understand attention to vocabulary in disciplinary teaching.

Development of the *Framework for the Analysis of Vocabulary LREs*

The *Framework* was developed on the basis of observations of LREs in classroom interaction in Accounting and Mathematics classes in a South Korean university setting (Hong, 2021b), a study which drew conceptually on earlier research into LREs in Accounting classroom interaction in New Zealand (Basturkmen & Shackleford, 2015). The development of the *Framework* was thus based on research into university classroom interaction in distinctive geographical settings.

The categories in the *Framework* and the research questions in the analysis were devised from our observations of the LREs. This was a largely inductive process in which we scrutinised the episodes in our attempt to identify the various aspects of lexical knowledge addressed. The procedure involved a reiterative process of examining, classifying, re-examining and reclassifying the vocabulary-focused LREs. To illustrate, when we examined the LREs, we noticed that whereas some LREs appeared to arise because classroom participants tried to make the meaning of lexical items clear, others appeared to serve to highlight lexical forms or which words could or should be used (lexical choice). In each case, the discourse topic shifted. In meaning-focused episodes, the discourse tended to shift from the form to the meaning of a word or expression, whereas in form-focused episodes the topic tended to shift from the meaning to the form. In lexical choice-focused episodes, the topic shifted from one to another, interchangeable lexical form. The observations led to the three-way classification scheme shown in Figure 3.1.

Category of lexical knowledge	Sub-categories	Examples
A Meaning LREs arise to deal with the meaning of a word/expression. Discourse topic often shifts from the form to the meaning of the word/expression. May include provision of a synonymous word/ expression or translation.	A1 Meaning of a single-word unit	**L: Adjusting** means getting used to, right? But in accounting it has a totally different meaning. . . **L: A deferral** means.. in Korean it's xxx
	A2 Meaning of a formulaic sequence (collocation)	**L: Cash basis accounting,** which means you get money, receive the money first. It's the practice of recording revenue when you receive cash first.

Figure 3.1 Framework for the analysis of vocabulary language-related episodes (LREs)

Framework for the Analysis of Vocabulary Language-Related 31

Category of lexical knowledge	Sub-categories	Examples
B Form LREs that arise to highlight or introduce words, word parts or expressions. Discourse topic often shifts from the meaning to the form of the word/word part/ expression.	B1 Single-word unit form	L: So, the process to determine the length of a curve is called **rectification**, right? S: **Decreasement**? L: Pretty close but **depreciation**
	B2 Formulaic sequence form (collocation)	L: What do we call this kind of expenditure paid in advance in an accounting period? S: **Prepaid expenses**. L: Yes, prepaid expense
	B3 Word part (root or affixes)	S: Account **payment**? L: Account **payable**
	B4 Sound-spelling correlate	L: We call it **notes** receivable **n-o-t-e-s**
C Lexical choice LREs that arise to highlight which words/expressions can or should be chosen.	C1 Alternatives, including abbreviations	L: Another name for this rule is **time period principle**, or you can say **periodicity assumption**. L: It's **Kronecker Delta** or just **Delta**
	C2 Coverage	L: Just use the term **expense**. It's a broader term. It covers much everything.
	C3 Preferred lexical choice Highlight a word/expression conventionally used in the disciplinary register or a more precise word/expression than one used in previous discourse.	L: You receive your **money** first. You receive your **revenue** first.

Figure 3.1 (Continued)

Attention to vocabulary items could be complex. To illustrate, in Example 3, the Lecturer draws attention to the meaning of "solvency". The Lecturer firstly provides a meaning ("the company's ability to pay the long-term debt or meet the obligations") and secondly provides the Korean translation. Example 5 is one LRE as it has one lexical target ("solvency"). It was classified as A1 according to the *Framework* as it focused on the meaning of a single unit item. Example 2 in the Introduction section includes two consecutive LREs, one targeting "net earnings" and one targeting "net income". There is discussion of an alternative lexical choice for "net earnings (C1) and the meaning of "net income", which was classified as A2 (meaning of a formulaic sequence).

Example 3

LECTURER: A company's liquidity and solvency and you know <u>solvency</u> means the company's ability to pay the long-term debt or meet the obligations. In Korean it's 지불상환능력

Application of the *Framework for the Analysis of Vocabulary LREs*

Setting and Data

EMI is becoming prevalent in South Korean university contexts (Byun & Kim, 2011). Here, as in some other Asian contexts, major drivers for the push towards EMI have been the internationalisation of higher education (Barnard & Hasim, 2019) and the desire to prepare students for global job opportunities. In South Korea, EMI allows universities to potentially attract greater numbers of students from neighbouring countries and beyond and help domestic students develop the English language skills they may require for future educational opportunities abroad. The potential of EMI to attract international students is a particularly important consideration in South Korea as the number of domestic students here is decreasing and some universities are expected to close in the short term (Chung, 2021).

The data comprised 180 vocabulary LREs from classroom interaction in four Accounting and four Mathematics university classes in a South Korean university (Hong, 2021b). These LREs were analysed to identify the relative proportion of episodes that addressed different types of vocabulary knowledge (meaning, form and lexical choice) and targeted single- or multi-word units. These were new forms of analysis that had not been considered in the earlier study.

The LREs were coded by the first researcher using categories from the *Framework* (cf. Figure 3.1) to answer the three research questions set out earlier. To check the reliability of the coding, 10% of the LREs were coded independently by the second researcher. The reliability score was 87.5%.

Findings

This analysis showed that the episodes addressed all three areas of lexical knowledge in the *Framework* with some regularity. Thus, a considerable

Framework for the Analysis of Vocabulary Language-Related 33

proportion of the LREs addressed each of the three areas of lexical knowledge. Overall, more episodes focused on meaning than form or lexical choice. However, as shown in Table 3.1, the relative proportion of LREs addressing the three areas varied in the two disciplines. In the Accounting classes, there was a predominance of meaning-focused LREs, whereas in the Mathematics classes, marginally more episodes addressed lexical choice than either meaning or form.

As shown in Table 3.2, a marginally higher proportion of meaning-focused LREs overall targeted single-unit lexical items. However, that proportion was greater in Mathematics compared to Accounting. Table 3.3 shows that although a greater proportion of form-focused LREs targeted single-word units in the Accounting classes, the reverse was the case in the Mathematics classes. LREs that addressed sound/spelling form issues were infrequent in both disciplines.

As shown in Table 3.4, almost half the meaning and form-focused LREs targeted multi-word units. The relative proportions were similar in both disciplines.

LREs that addressed lexical choice mainly served to provide alternative words and terms (see Table 3.5). Slightly under a third of lexical choice LREs appeared to signal a preferred (more sophisticated or register-appropriate) choice. Example 4 illustrates an alternative lexical choice as the Lecturer provides two alternatives but does not signal either one as being a preferred choice. In Example 5, the Lecturer corrects the student's use of the word "money" and provides the term "cash" presumably to signal it as being a more appropriate choice for Accounting register.

Table 3.1 Distribution of categories of focus by discipline

	Meaning	*Form*	*Lexical choice*	*Total*
Accounting	79 (56.8%)	26 (18.7%)	34 (24.4%)	139
Mathematics	11 (26.8%)	14 (34.1%)	16 (39%)	41
	90 (50%)	40 (22.2%)	50 (27.7%)	180

Table 3.2 Sub-types of meaning-focused LREs by discipline

	Meaning of a single-unit word	*Meaning of a formulaic sequence*	*Total*
Accounting	45 (56.9%)	34 (43%)	79
Mathematics	8 (72.7%)	3 (27.2%)	11
	53 (58.8%)	37 (41.1%)	90

Table 3.3 Sub-types of form-focused LREs by discipline

	Single-unit form	Formulaic sequence form	Word part	Sound-spelling correlate	Total
Accounting	10 (38.4%)	9 (34.6%)	6 (23.0%)	1 (3.8%)	26
Mathematics	2 (14.2%)	6 (42.8%)	4 (28.5%)	2 (14.2%)	14
	12 (30%)	15 (37.5%)	10 (25%)	3 (7.5%)	40

Table 3.4 Targets of LREs by discipline

	Single-word units	Multi-word units	Total
Accounting	55 (56%)	43 (44%)	98
Mathematics	10 (53%)	9 (47%)	19
	65 (55.5%)	52 (44.5%)	117

*Category A & B LREs

Table 3.5 Sub-types of lexical choice-focused LREs by discipline

	Alternatives	Coverage	Preferred lexical choice	Total
Accounting	20 (58.8%)	1 (2.9%)	13 (38.2%)	34
Mathematics	15 (93.7%)	0	1 (6.2%)	16
	35 (70%)	1 (2%)	14 (28%)	50

Example 4

LECTURER: Well in that case you can just use <u>liability</u> instead of <u>debt.</u> They are synonyms, so you can use either in this case.

Example 5

LECTURER: And cash accounting?
STUDENT: Just <u>money.</u>
LECTURER: Yes, focusing on the <u>cash.</u>

Discussion of Findings

That attention to vocabulary was spread across all three areas of lexical knowledge (meaning, form and lexical choice) was not entirely predictable.

Anecdotally, it is often reported that content lecturers deal mainly with the meaning of vocabulary. Our findings indicated that a good proportion of LREs in the South Korean university setting highlighted or introduced lexical forms and lexical choices. This finding suggests that in this context classroom interaction provided wide- rather than narrow-angled support for students' development of lexical knowledge. The lecturers were not by any stretch only concerned with meaning. That the topic of lexical choice was regularly addressed in the interaction appears to provide support for findings from previous stimulated recall-based inquiry which reported lecturers' aims to introduce words and expressions which could be used interchangeably in their discipline (Basturkmen, 2018).

Discussions of vocabulary meaning or form regularly concerned single- and multi-unit lexical units, and only a slightly higher proportion of the LREs concerned single-word units. It was thus clear that the Korean EMI classroom participants were as concerned with formulaic sequences (multi-word units) as with single-word units. This finding would appear to underscore the importance of academic and disciplinary collocations highlighted in recent corpus-analytical research (Green & Lambert, 2018; Simpson-Vlach & Ellis, 2010). The collocations targeted by the LREs were generally either terms for key disciplinary concepts, such as "periodic function" (Mathematics), or conventionalised expressions, such as "we say 'to streamline assets'" (Accounting). It seems that the classroom discourse regularly highlighted the kind of formulaic sequences that could enable students to express complete ideas in ways that are likely to be correctly interpreted as described earlier by Wray (2021).

The acquisition of vocabulary can seem to be a vast task. Whereas there is a finite set of grammar structures to be learnt, there is a seemingly endless set of vocabulary items, even in the context of the learning of a disciplinary register. It was pleasing to see that on occasion the lecturers highlighted prefixes in the word forms they discussed. By highlighting such word parts, the lecturers appeared to provide lexical information that students might apply when trying to understand other unfamiliar words or construct new word+ forms in the future. See Example 6 from a Mathematics class. Here, the Lecturer draws attention to the prefix "bi-":

Example 6

LECTURER: What happens when we multiply a binomial by itself then?
(Silence)
LECTURER: Okay, so we call this work binomial theorem. Okay binomial theorem or binominal expression. Because this <u>prefix (bi-) means two</u>.

Finally, although the vocabulary LREs in the South Korean university classrooms were brief, transitory interludes within the classroom discourse that was primarily oriented to the discussion of conceptual content, they nevertheless could be multifaceted and include more than one category from the *Framework*. To illustrate, the Lecturer in Example 6 highlights a word form ("we call this work binomial theorem"), provides an alternative lexical choice ("or binomial expression") and highlights a word part ("this prefix bi") all within the same turn in the interaction. See also the commentary on our observations of multiple categories from the *Framework* in Examples 2 and 3.

Suggestions for Researchers and Lecturers

Other researchers, teachers and lecturers may find the *Framework* of value in their reflections or research into the role that incidental attention to vocabulary plays in EMI classroom interaction. Above, we illustrated use of the *Framework* in a quantitative analysis of a data set and we hope it provided a concrete procedure that can be adopted or adapted.

The aims of our analysis earlier were descriptive only, and we did not include any inferential statistics to search for possible disciplinary variation. However, other researchers might want to conduct cross-disciplinary comparative studies and include tests of statistic inference. There has been considerable interest in disciplinary variation in discourse features in recent years. However, it is also possible that classroom interaction transcends disciplinary variation. An analysis of linguistic features of professors' questions across three disciplinary class settings found similarities rather than differences (Chang, 2012), which may suggest that the extent of disciplinary differences reported for academic writing is less evident in interactive academic speaking (Basturkmen, 2021; Chang, 2012).

A recent international survey of EMI (Sahan et al., 2021) draws attention to the professional teaching development needs of EMI lecturers:

> Professional development opportunities appear to be limited for teaching staff on EMI programmes. When support is offered to lecturers, it tends to focus on improving teachers' general English proficiency, not improving the skills required to teach in English in a multi-/bilingual classroom context.
>
> (p. 8)

The *Framework* (cf. Figure 3.1) could be used by disciplinary lecturers or by trainers in professional development workshops to guide the lecturers' reflections on or observations of the ways they attend incidentally to vocabulary during classroom interaction. Disciplinary lecturers could draw on the categories in the *Framework* to classify excerpts in recordings or transcripts of interaction in their classes. Such reflection may raise their awareness of elements of their teaching practice that often go unnoticed in real-time interaction. Novice disciplinary lecturers might find it of interest to examine excerpts in recordings or transcripts of any experienced colleagues (who are willing) to offer them a window into their practice. The excerpts could show in a concrete way how experienced colleagues deal with vocabulary as it arises in the context of classroom interaction. Often it is only planned teaching practices, such as prepared materials, that are made available for others to observe. A good deal can be learnt, however, from observation of how experienced lecturers manage vocabulary questions and difficulties in real time.

Finally, researchers could draw on the *Framework* to investigate the amount or type of incidental attention to vocabulary in classrooms across various settings, such as tertiary versus secondary educational settings, tertiary year-one classes (when lecturers may pay particular attention to dealing with the *new* vocabulary of the discipline) versus classes in later years of study, or to analyse students' questions about vocabulary or what lecturers select to correct in their students' use of vocabulary in disciplinary classrooms.

References

Barnard, R., & Hasim, Z. (2019). *English-medium instruction programmes: Perspectives from South Asian universities*. Routledge.
Basturkmen, H. (2018). Dealing with language issues during subject teaching in EMI: The perspectives of two accounting lecturers. *TESOL Quarterly*, *52*(3), 692–700.
Basturkmen, H. (2021). *Linguistic description in English for academic purposes*. Routledge.
Basturkmen, H., & Shackleford, N. (2015). How content lecturers help students with language: An observational study of language-related episodes in interaction in first year accounting classrooms. *English for Specific Purposes*, *37*(1), 87–97.
Byun, K. Y., & Kim, M. J. (2011). Shifting patterns of the Government's policies for the internationalization of Korean higher education. *Journal of Studies in International Education*, *15*(5), 467–486.
Chang, Y-Y. (2012). The use of questions by professors in lectures given in English: Influences of disciplinary cultures. *English for Specific Purposes*, *31*, 103–116.
Chung, A. (2021, May 29). 'Zombie universities' face drastic actions as births fall. *University World News*. www.universityworldnews.com/post.php?story=20210528105651120
Costa, F. (2012). Focus on form in ICLHE lectures in Italy. *AILA Review*, *25*, 30–47.

Coxhead, A. (2018). Replication research in pedagogical approaches to formulaic sequences: Jones & Haywood (2004), and Alali & Schmitt (2012). *Language Teaching*, *51*(1), 113–123.

Doiz, A., & Lasagabaster, D. (2021). Analyzing EMI teachers' and students' talk about language. In D. Lasagabaster & A. Doiz (Eds.), *Language use in English-medium instruction at university: International perspectives on teacher practice* (pp. 34–55). Routledge.

Ellis, R. (1994). *Implicit and explicit learning of languages*. Academic Press.

Green, C., & Lambert, J. (2018). Position vectors, homologous chromosomes and gamma rays: Promoting disciplinary literacy through secondary phrase lists. *English for Specific Purposes*, *53*(1), 1–12.

Hong, J. (2021a). Incidental attention to language during disciplinary teaching: An observation study of LREs in a first-year EMI computer programming lecture. *Asia-Pacific LSP & Professional Communication Association News*, *3*, 9–12. www.lsppc.org/archives

Hong, J. (2021b). *Attention to language in EMI in high school and university settings is South Korea* (Doctoral dissertation). University of Auckland.

Hong, J., & Basturkmen, H. (2020). Incidental attention to academic language during content teaching in two EMI classes in South Korean high schools. *Journal of English for Academic Purposes*, *48*. https://doi.org/10.1016/j.jeap.2020.100921

Horst, M., Cobb, T., & Meara, P. (1998). Beyond a clockwork orange: Acquiring second language vocabulary through reading. *Reading in a Foreign Language*, *11*(2), 207–223.

Hulstijin, J. (2001). Intention and incidental second language vocabulary learning: A reappraisal of elaboration, rehearsal, and automaticity. In P. Robinson (Ed.), *Cognition and second language instruction* (pp. 258–286). Cambridge University Press.

Martinez, R., Machado, P., & Palma, C. (2021). An exploratory analysis of language-related episodes (LREs) in a Brazilian context. In D. Lasagabaster & A. Doiz (Eds.), *Language use in English-medium instruction at university: International perspectives on teacher practice* (pp. 11–33). Routledge.

McLaughlin, E., & Parkinson, J. (2018). 'We learn as we go': How acquisition of a technical vocabulary is supported during vocational training. *English for Specific Purposes*, *50*, 14–27.

Nation, P. (2001). *Learning vocabulary in another language*. Cambridge University Press.

Rot, S. (2013). Incidental vocabulary acquisition. In C. A. Chapelle (Ed.), *The encyclopedia of applied linguistics (2632–2640)*. Wiley-Blackwell. doi:10.1002/9781405198431.wbeal0531

Sahan, K. (2021). In conversation with Ernesto Macaro on English-medium instruction. *Regional English Language Council Journal*, *52*(2), 334–341.

Sahan, K., Mikolajewska, A., Rose, H., Macaro, E., Searler, M., Aizawa, I., Zhou, S., & Veitch, A. (2021). *Global mapping of English-medium instruction in higher education 2020 and beyond*. The British Council.

Simpson-Vlach, R., & Ellis, N. C. (2010). An academic formulas list: New methods in phraseology research. *Applied Linguistics*, *31*(4), 497–512.

Swain, M., & Lapkin, S. (1998). Interaction and second language learning. Two adolescent French immersion learners working together. *The Modern Language Journal*, *82*(3), 320–337.

Wray, A. (2021). Formulaic sequences. In C. A. Chapelle (Ed.), *The encyclopedia of applied linguistics (2200–2205)*. Wiley-Blackwell.

4 Features of Spoken Input Across the Disciplines and at the Interface Between English-Medium Instruction and Disciplinary Discourse

Cristina Mariotti

Introduction

As English-Medium Instruction (EMI) programmes are spreading throughout Europe, stakeholders are increasingly developing an awareness about the need to address the professional development of lecturers to help them face the challenges posed by the introduction of an L2 as the language of instruction (Guarda & Helm, 2016). In particular, avoiding knowledge pauperisation represents a crucial element of L2-mediated instruction especially at university level, where preserving the quality and quantity of content is fundamental to safeguard the preparation of future professionals. It is therefore important to reflect both on content and on delivery of the input students are exposed to while attending lectures firstly because lectures are the predominant speech event in university instruction, and secondly because during teacher-fronted lectures students are exposed to extensive amounts of spoken language (more than 75% of class time is usually taken up by the instructor according to Dafouz et al., 2007), which represents one of the main drives of familiarisation with the discourse of the discipline they have chosen to study.

At the same time, though, it should be noted that EMI lecturers often think they have nothing to do with the language being used as the medium of instruction, that is the "E" in EMI, let alone be responsible for correcting or teaching it (Airey, 2011; Doiz & Lasagabaster, 2020) for the most diverse reasons: typically because they are busy professionals or because the change from teaching in their L1 to teaching in English was not their choice, but they were thrown in at the deep end to satisfy the need for more English-taught courses imposed by their institutions' internationalisation policies (Airey, 2011; Costa & Coleman, 2013). Nevertheless, even if they refuse to consider themselves involved in language teaching, content lecturers are still invested with the task of helping their students develop disciplinary literacy as "it is a fallacy to think that content and language can be separated in this way – content and language are inextricably entwined" (Airey, 2016, p. 93). Moreover, Costa (2012) has shown that content lecturers who declare that they have nothing to do with language teaching unconsciously produce input that contains attention to the language used as the medium of instruction, such as the use of pre-emptive focus on form.

To provide insights into how lecturers might attain greater awareness of their input presentation strategies, in the present chapter, EMI research describing the spoken input produced in teacher-fronted lectures in settings where English was used as the vehicle for instruction will be reviewed with the aim of identifying recurring, cross-disciplinary strategies that increase input comprehensibility. Moreover, the intersection between these strategies and disciplinary discourse will be explored to show how lecturers can exploit this synergy to foster content acquisition in a way that is epistemologically appropriate and effective.

Scope and Aims of This Chapter

The literature investigating spoken input in EMI lectures was reviewed to answer the following questions: (1) Is it possible to identify recurring features that characterise the speech delivered by lecturers in EMI settings regardless of the discipline being taught (transversal input presentation strategies)? (2) How does the spoken input produced by lecturers in EMI settings reflect discipline-specific discourse features?

In order to answer the first research question, a qualitative analysis was carried out based on the following criteria: relevant data were selected from research providing descriptions of the input produced in universities across the European area where English is used as the medium of instruction by non-native speaking content lecturers teaching in countries where English is not the native language. The Google Scholar database was searched using combinations of the words "disciplin*", "effective", "English-medium", "input", "L1-L2", "lectur*", "spoken" and "strateg*".

To answer the second research question, studies on the spoken input of lecturers in EMI settings were taken into consideration in order to detect as many manifestations of disciplinary discourse as possible. The retrieved papers were double-checked by another researcher for consistency with the selection criteria. The main limitation of this study is represented by the fact that due to the high variability of the lexis that can be used to refer to linguistic input, the search results might be incomplete. For these reasons, the present research cannot be described as systematic and no generalisations can be drawn from the reviewed data.

Input Presentation Strategies in EMI Lectures Across the Disciplines

Even if a certain degree of variation can be determined by the individual teaching style of a lecturer and by local, cultural norms, teacher-fronted lectures are for the most part monologic events (Anderson & Ciliberti, 2002) characterised by a division into codified macro and micro phases (Young, 1994) with a focus on conveying disciplinary content. In this type of speech events, exchanges between lecturers and students are typically scarce and limited to specific, designated sequences, for instance, after the presentation of a topic or at the end of the lecture (Hansen & Jensen, 1994). This is also due to the large size of the audience that is typical of traditional, ex-cathedra lectures, which increases the already existent asymmetry between participants and makes it even more challenging for students to initiate interaction sequences.

At the same time, though, lectures are socially situated communicative events where lecturers are called to accomplish the task of creating rapport, maintaining the attention of students and facilitating their comprehension and acquisition of disciplinary content and disciplinary discourse (since the two cannot be separated). From a linguistic point of view, lecturers try to carry out this complex task in many ways, for instance, asking several types of questions (Crawford Camiciottoli, 2005; Thompson, 1998), expressing stance through the use of the inclusive "we" (Fortanet-Gómez, 2004; Hansen & Jensen, 1994), producing speech rich in rephrasing and examples (Flowerdew & Miller, 1997), and using discourse markers and signposting (Chaudron & Richards, 1986; Flowerdew & Miller, 1997). Young (1994), in particular, stresses the importance of making information clearly accessible to students and underlines the relevance of redundancy and explicitness for academic didactic spoken discourse.

In EMI settings, the use of an L2 as the language of instruction introduces yet another fundamental variable which makes comprehension even more stringent as understanding the language is the necessary requisite for content processing and acquisition. In other words, with respect to L1-taught lectures, EMI lecturers must shift from a teacher-centred practice to a more student-centred one, developing an awareness of the possible linguistic difficulties of their students, most of whom are studying in a foreign language and thus may need support and guidance to access and negotiate knowledge (Klaassen & De Graaff, 2001).

Thus, it can be assumed that comprehension-enhancing strategies such as signposting, redundancy and a higher degree of interactivity are frequently produced overall in EMI settings and, in particular, they are more frequently produced by lecturers in EMI settings than in L1-taught ones. In the following paragraphs, these assumptions will be tested by reviewing studies that have investigated these strategies across disciplines in EMI programmes. Findings will be organised around the themes of explicitness, interaction and student-centred teaching, paying particular attention to contrastive studies analysing the speech produced by the same lecturer teaching the same content in their L1 and in English.

Explicitness

Literature comparing changes in the input produced by lecturers when teaching EMI courses as opposed to courses taught in their L1 reports mixed findings. In the Netherlands, Vinke (1995) analysed 16 Engineering lecturers teaching in English and Dutch and found that they tend to use structuring techniques such as signposting more frequently in English than in Dutch, but they are less redundant in English. For most of the lecturers, the speech rate is reduced by an average of 17% when they speak in English. In partial contrast with these findings, Dafouz Milne and Núñez Perucha (2010) analysed contrastively six lectures given by Engineering lecturers in Spanish (L1) and English (L2) revealing that L1-medium lectures contained more explicit signalling, a wider variety of stylistic choices, and a higher use of interaction devices and conclusion markers, and concluded that non-native lecturers need to be trained to use these strategies also in EMI (2010).

Thøgersen and Airey (2011) analysed five Science lectures (three in Danish and two in English) given by the same lecturer, finding that the lecturer took longer to present the same subject matter in English, speaking more slowly, using more repetitions in L2 and more formal language, similar to written, textbook style. Similar results were obtained by Arkin and Osam (2015), who conducted a study on a lecturer teaching the same content in Turkish and in English to undergraduate university students studying Human Resources Management at an English-medium university in Turkey. Findings show that on average in the EMI course the lecturer took 11% more time to present the same content in English. Moreover, he tended to use self-repetitions most of the time in a conscious effort to help comprehension. The authors argue that this might negatively affect the quality of subject matter learning as the lecturer was not able to cover the intended amount of content. Costa and Mariotti (2017) observed differences in content presentation in the input produced by the same lecturer teaching Economics in EMI versus Italian-taught classes, showing that in the EMI class the lecturer tended to produce more signposting and structuring speech to help the students orient themselves throughout the lecture; to be more redundant and semantically clear by means of repetitions, paraphrases and examples; and to adopt a slower speech rate in a conscious effort to adapt her teaching style to increase input comprehensibility and help students process the content by making the language more explicit. This lecturer managed to cover the same amount of content in both classes, thus contrasting the findings of Arkin and Osam (2015).

Molino (2017) found that the speech of six Italian L1 lecturers teaching Physical Sciences and Engineering at a Northern Italian university contains more repeats (i.e. exact repetitions of single words or short sequences that characterise spoken language performance) than one would expect in spoken native English. This can give an impression of reduced fluency, but Molino observes that not only do repeats not affect understanding, but they "may even be functional to message processing" (2017, p. 200) in EMI settings as they give students time to orient themselves throughout the lecture and to manage their high-attention processing activity more efficiently. Reformulations, instead, were used to make information more accessible, to increase the accuracy of the message, to present students with specialised terminology, and to socialise them into the communities and values of the discipline (2017).

Even if the empirical results reviewed show some discrepancies, we can safely assume that discursive differences such as greater redundancy and explicitness and slower speech rate in the speech produced by lecturers across disciplines are distinctive features of EMI contexts.

Interaction

Interaction has increasingly been recognised as an important factor in English-taught lectures as it activates and facilitates the learning process while balancing asymmetrical roles through signs of cooperation and identification with the audience (Crawford Camiciottoli, 2004; Flowerdew & Miller, 1997; Morell, 2004; Sánchez García, 2010). Questions, in particular, have always been an important interactional tool used by lecturers to activate and facilitate the learning process. In spite of their relevance for facilitating input comprehension, only few studies have focused on the frequency of use and the type of questions produced by lecturers in EMI settings, and even fewer have investigated differences between the input produced by the same speaker in EMI lectures and in lectures where participants share the L1 used as the medium of instruction.

Dafouz Milne and Sánchez García (2013) described the use of questions across disciplines (Business, Engineering and Physics) in three different Spanish universities. They report that questions are indeed used in English-Medium Instruction lectures, the most recurrently used by the observed lecturers being confirmation checks, followed by self-answered questions and display questions. These findings suggest that these strategies are produced in EMI across disciplines and that "lectures in an educational setting seem to transcend the academic disciplinary culture and exhibit certain uniformity or what we have called a common macro-structure" (2013, p. 144).

Bier (2020) analysed the pragmatic strategies used by lecturers teaching Mathematics, Computer Science, Management, Economics and Chemistry to enhance their communicative effectiveness while lecturing in English at a public university in Northern Italy and found that questions, in particular confirmation checks (referred to as "rhetorical questions" in her article), are the lecturers' most favourite pragmatic tool to involve the audience and receive feedback.

Concerning research on the input produced by the same speaker in EMI and in L1-taught lectures, Vinke (1995) found that student–lecturer interactions occur more frequently when lecturers teach in English, even if in both contexts they held turns almost exclusively. In the same line of research, Costa and Mariotti (2017) observed that as far as the degree of interactivity is concerned, in the EMI class the lecturer tended to ask more display questions, to which students reacted more often than their L1-taught counterparts and conclude that the observed EMI class shows a higher degree of interactivity.

Thus, even if we need to acquire more data in this domain, the reviewed results suggest that in EMI settings lecturers tend to produce more interaction-fostering strategies than they would in an L1-taught class.

Student-Centred Teaching

Explicitness and interaction can be seen as part of a wider tendency in EMI teaching methodology which consists in a change from a predominantly teacher-led to a more student-centred approach (Guarda & Helm, 2016). This shift may be necessary and beneficial in EMI contexts where decentring the focus of pedagogic action from the instructor to the students might make students more involved in the co-construction of knowledge and might give them greater possibilities to voice their difficulties and receive support and guidance to access and negotiate knowledge (Klaassen & De Graaff, 2001).

For instance, Klaassen (2001) studied the relationship between lecture intelligibility and the language competence and pedagogical approach of the lecturers in EMI teaching in a technical university in the Netherlands. The findings show that student-centred lecturing, characterised by the fact that lectures were organised around student presentations and discussions, is a much more important factor in the success of a lecture than the lecturer's language competence.

From the point of view of language management, it has been observed that lecturer speech showing an inclusive stance can reflect a more student-centred methodology and that lecturers can use it to signal that they are willing to depart from an ex-cathedra approach to teaching to incorporate the contribution of students in the speech event. Dafouz et al. (2007) investigated the use of personal pronouns and modal verbs in the spoken productions of three lecturers in the Faculty of Aeronautical Engineering at the Universidad Politécnica de Madrid (UPM). They describe the use of the inclusive "we" as being pervasive and indicative of lecturers adopting a role of cooperation and identification with the audience, whereas "I" was used for direct reference and "you" was used to address illustrative generalisations (2007, p. 658). Two modal verb phrases, namely "we can" and "we have to", are among the most frequently produced verbal clusters. The former is used not only to express possibility or permission but also to open up space for negotiation, while the latter appears to have no connotation of obligation but is rather used to present the steps that need to be followed in the scientific line of reasoning. The authors conclude that by using these input presentation strategies the observed lecturers are making themselves more accessible to students. Similar findings were obtained by Molino (2018) in her analysis of six lectures held in English at a large university in Northern Italy by Italian native speakers teaching Physical Sciences and Engineering. In these lectures, "we", which is the most frequent personal pronoun in the corpus, is used as a metadiscourse marker to guide the audience in reviewing and previewing discourse organisation by engaging and bonding with them (2018, p. 936).

It might be argued that adopting a student-centred approach, using strategies that increase explicitness, and fostering interaction in the classroom are not unique features of English-mediated instruction since these are simply best practices for any type of teaching (Björkman, 2010) and "changing the lecturing language merely accentuates communication problems that are already present in first-language lectures" (Airey & Linder, 2006, p. 559).

Costa and Mariotti (2021) agree that these strategies can raise awareness and change traditional ways of lecturing no matter what language is used and could indeed be applied to good teaching practices in general, but at the same time, they observe that they are particularly suitable and more likely to be found in settings where an L2 is used as the medium of instruction as they specifically call for strategies that can make input more comprehensible regardless of the discipline being taught.

Discipline-Specific Input Presentation Strategies in EMI

There is general agreement that the disciplinary differences in epistemological beliefs and knowledge structures affect the use of language and the teaching approach of lecturers (Becher, 1989; Hyland, 2000; Neumann & Becher, 2002). Thus, following Airey and Linder (2009), it is held that each discipline has its own unique order of discourse "so that the order of discourse of, say, art history, will be radically different than the order of discourse of physics" (2009, p. 2).

Concerning the description of discipline-specific input presentation strategies in EMI settings, the research conducted in the present study evidenced a paucity of studies addressing the spoken productions of lecturers. One of them is represented by an investigation of the input produced by an English native speaker in an L2-medium teaching context at an Italian university (Crawford Camiciottoli, 2005), where it is observed that the conventional discourse features of some disciplines can create problems for L2 listeners, as in the case of Economics, where metaphors are central to the expression of basic concepts. In particular, two macro metaphors permeate the discourse of the discipline: economy as a machine or moving vehicle that "starts up", "slows down" or "accelerates", and economy as a living organism that "grows", "suffers" or "flourishes". Since these metaphors are pervasive in the disciplinary discourse of Economics, the author suggests that the related terms should play a key role in the vocabulary acquisition of L2 business and economics students. An awareness of the students' comprehension difficulties might therefore activate what we refer to as the discipline/EMI methodology interface, where explicitness strategies are applied to a discipline-specific feature of academic spoken English.

Bowles (2017) reports an occurrence of disciplinary variation in the speech produced by lecturers and students during oral examinations of Immunology in an English-taught undergraduate Medicine programme in Italy. It is relevant to comment on the findings of this study because they have implications for how lecturers shape their input during lectures as conducive to the right approach that students need to adopt for the examination. During examinations, Italian lecturers expect students to adopt a narrative framework where they reconstruct and co-construct immunological processes step by step using precise terminology and process verbs. English native-speaking students taking this exam experience difficulties in spite of their command of the language because they adopt the framework expected by Medicine lecturers in Anglophone settings, where medical students are presented with clinical problems and are asked to find solutions, working backwards from the problem in written form. This difference is determined by culture-specific disciplinary variation intertwined with a more emic type of variation consisting in the local structuring of the medical syllabus. As a matter of fact, unlike what happens in Italy, in Anglophone countries, the Immunology course is not part of the undergraduate programme and is taught from a strong clinical perspective. An awareness of these differences would imply the activation of the discipline/EMI interface whereby lecturers could pre-emptively make the expected sequence clear during lectures and could scaffold the oral productions of students maximising the efficacy and the impact of the learning process.

Discussion and Conclusions

To answer the first research question ("Is it possible to identify features that characterise the spoken input delivered by lecturers in EMI settings regardless of the discipline being taught?"), it seems that signposting, redundancy expressed through repetitions, paraphrases and examples, a higher degree of interactivity, and a slower speech rate seem to be more frequently produced in EMI than in L1-taught lectures by lecturers who teach the same content in both settings. These strategies have been observed across disciplines and may be distinctive of EMI not because they are found exclusively in the speech of lecturers teaching in English but because they are more likely to make input more comprehensible when an L2 is used as the medium of instruction. Concerning the second research question ("How does spoken input produced by lecturers in EMI settings reflect discipline-specific discourse features?"), two instances of disciplinary discourse in EMI settings were highlighted, represented by the use of a specific kind of metaphor in the case of Economics and the choice of a narrative sequence instead of a problem-solving approach in the case of Medicine. These examples provide further evidence that language and content are intertwined and that this knowledge can be exploited to the advantage of learners. By recognising the lecture as the space where EMI methodology and disciplinary literacy intersect, lecturers can become more conscious of features that characterise effective teaching in L2-mediated instruction and can deploy input presentation strategies that are tailored to increase students' awareness and construction of disciplinary knowledge. In other words, lecturers could increase the effectiveness of their teaching by incorporating in their practice explicitness-fostering strategies, interaction and, in general, a more student-centred approach honing their ability to select the most appropriate strategies based on the requirements of the particular discourse of a discipline, or even of its local epistemology. In order to foster this process, EMI research should investigate and describe the intersection between EMI methodology and disciplinary discourse in the spoken productions of lecturers more systematically.

English language proficiency is indeed a relevant prerequisite, but reflection on teaching methodology should be playing an equally important role in lecturer training programmes since the interplay between language and methodology allows lecturers to convey content without simplifying it and to co-construct disciplinary discourse together with their students. As Guarda and Helm put it, "it is the disruption caused by the introduction of a foreign language for teaching and learning that can offer opportunities for reflection and innovation in pedagogy" (2016, p. 13). In this sense, EMI can be seen as a magnifying lens, an amplifying device, making teaching issues more evident and therefore more effectively manageable.

References

Airey, J. (2011). Talking about teaching in English: Swedish university lecturers' experiences of changing teaching language. *Iberica*, 22, 35–54.
Airey, J. (2016). EAP, EMI or CLIL? In K. Hyland & P. Shaw (Eds.), *The Routledge handbook of English for academic purposes* (pp. 71–83). Routledge.
Airey, J., & Linder, C. (2006). Language and the experience of learning university physics in Sweden. *European Journal of Physics*, 27, 553–560.
Airey, J., & Linder, C. (2009). A disciplinary discourse perspective on university science learning: Achieving fluency in a critical constellation of modes. *Journal of Research in Science Teaching*, 46(1), 27–49.
Anderson, L., & Ciliberti, A. (2002). Monologicità e di(a)logicità nella comunicazione accademica. In C. Bazzanella (Ed.), *Sul Dialogo. Contesti e Forme di Interazione Verbale* (pp. 92–105). Guerini Studio.
Arkin, E., & Osam, N. (2015). English-medium higher education: A case study in a Turkish university context. In S. Dimova, A. K. Hultgren, & C. Jensen (Eds.), *English-medium instruction in European higher education* (pp. 177–199). De Gruyter Mouton.
Becher, T. (1989). *Academic tribes and territories: Intellectual enquiry and the cultures of disciplines*. SRHE/Open University Press.

Bier, A. (2020). On the interplay between strategic competence and language competence in lecturing through English. Findings from Italy. *EL.LE*, *9*(3), 345–366.

Bowles, H. (2017). Immunologically speaking: Oral examinations, ELF and EMI. *Lingue e Linguaggi*, *24*, 185–201.

Björkman, B. (2010). 'So you think you can ELF'. English as a Lingua Franca as the medium of instruction. *Hermes*, *45*, 77–96.

Chaudron, C., & Richards, J. (1986). The effect of discourse markers on the comprehension of lectures. *Applied Linguistics*, *7*(2), 113–125.

Costa, F. (2012). Evidence from English-medium science lectures by native speakers of Italian. In U. Smit & E. Dafouz (Eds.), *Integrating content and language in higher education: Gaining insights into English-medium instruction at European universities* (pp. 30–47). AILA Review, 25.

Costa, F., & Coleman, J. A. (2013). A survey of English-medium instruction in Italian higher education. *International Journal of Bilingual Education and Bilingualism*, *16*(1), 3–19.

Costa, F., & Mariotti, C. (2017). Differences in content presentation and learning outcomes in English-medium instruction (EMI) vs. Italian-medium instruction (IMI) contexts. In J. Valcke & R. Wilkinson (Eds.), *Integrating content and language in higher education* (pp. 187–204). Peter Lang.

Costa, F., & Mariotti, C. (2021). Strategies to enhance comprehension in EMI lectures: Examples from the Italian context. In A. Doiz & D. Lasagabaster (Eds.), *Global perspectives on language aspects and teacher development in English-medium instruction* (pp. 80–99). Routledge.

Crawford Camiciottoli, B. (2004). Interactive discourse structuring in L2 guest lectures: Some insights from a comparative corpus-based study. *Journal of English for Academic Purposes*, *3*(1), 39–54.

Crawford Camiciottoli, B. (2005). Adjusting a business lecture for an international audience. A case study. *English for Specific Purposes*, *24*(2), 183–199.

Dafouz Milne, E., & Núñez Perucha, B. (2010). Metadiscursive devices in university lectures. A contrastive analysis of L1 and L2 teacher performance. In C. Dalton Puffer, T. Nikula, & U. Smit (Eds.), *Language use and language learning in CLIL classrooms* (pp. 213–232). AILA Applied Linguistics Series, 7.

Dafouz Milne, E., Núñez Perucha, B., & Sancho, C. (2007). Analysing stance in a CLIL university context: Non-native speaker use of personal pronouns and modal verbs. *International Journal of Bilingual Education and Bilingualism*, *10*(5), 647–662.

Dafouz Milne, E., & Sánchez García, D. (2013). 'Does everybody understand?' Teacher questions across disciplines in English-mediated university lectures: An exploratory study. *Language Value*, *5*(1), 129–151.

Doiz, A., & Lasagabaster, D. (2020). Dealing with language issues in English-medium instruction at university: A comprehensive approach. *International Journal of Bilingual Education and Bilingualism*, *23*(3), 257–262.

Flowerdew, J., & Miller, L. (1997). The teaching of academic listening comprehension and the question of authenticity. *English for Specific Purposes*, *16*(1), 27–46.

Fortanet-Gómez, I. (2004). Enhancing the speaker-audience relationship in academic lectures. In P. Garcés, R. Gómez Moron, L. Fernández, & M. Padilla (Eds.), *Current trends in intercultural, cognitive and social pragmatics* (pp. 83–96). Editorial Kronos.

Guarda, M., & Helm, F. (2016). 'I have discovered new teaching pathways'. The link between language shift and teaching practice. *International Journal of Bilingual Education and Bilingualism*, *20*(7), 897–913.

Hansen, C., & Jensen, C. (1994). Evaluating lecture comprehension. In J. Flowerdew (Ed.), *Academic listening: Research perspectives* (pp. 241–268). Cambridge University Press.

Hyland, K. (2000). *Disciplinary discourses: Social interactions in academic writing*. University of Michigan Press.

Klaassen, R. G. (2001). *The international university curriculum: Challenges in English-medium engineering education* (Doctoral dissertation). Technische Universitat Delft. http://repository.tudelft.nl/view/ir/uuid%3Adea78484-b8c2-40d0-9677-6a508878e3d9/

Klaassen, R. G., & de Graaff, E. (2001). Facing innovation: Preparing lecturers for English-medium instruction in a non-native context. *European Journal of Engineering Education*, *26*(3), 281–289.

Molino, A. (2017). Repetition and rephrasing in physical sciences and engineering English-medium lectures in Italy. In C. Boggio & A. Molino (Eds.), *English in Italy: Linguistic, educational and professional challenges* (pp. 182–202). FrancoAngeli.

Molino, A. (2018). 'What I'm Speaking is almost English . . . ': A corpus-based study of metadiscourse in English-medium lectures at an Italian university. *Educational Sciences: Theory and Practice*, *18*(4), 935 956.

Morell, T. (2004). Interactive lecture discourse for university EFL students. *English for Specific Purposes*, *23*(3), 325–338. https://doi.org/10.1016/s0889-4906(03)00029-2

Neumann, R., & Becher, T. (2002). Teaching and learning in their disciplinary contexts: A conceptual analysis. *Studies in Higher Education*, *27*(4), 405–417.

Sánchez García, D. (2010). *Classroom interaction in university settings: The case of questions in three disciplines* (M.A. Thesis). Universidad Complutense de Madrid. http://eprints.ucm.es/12793/1/Davinia_Sanchez.pdf

Thøgersen, J., & Airey, J. (2011). Lecturing undergraduate science in Danish and in English: A comparison of speaking rate and rhetorical style. *English for Specific Purposes*, *30*(3), 209–221.

Thompson, S. (1998). Why ask questions in a monologue? Language choices at work in scientific and linguistic talk. In S. Hunston (Ed.), *Language at work* (pp. 137–150). Multilingual Matters.

Vinke, A. A. (1995). *English as the medium of instruction in Dutch engineering education* (Doctoral dissertation). Technische Universiteit Delft.

Young, L. (1994). University lectures. Macrostructure and microfeatures. In J. Flowerdew (Ed.), *Academic listening: Research perspectives* (pp. 159–176). Cambridge University Press.

5 Materials Design for the Development of Subject-Specific Literacies in English-Taught Courses at University

Cynthia Pimentel Velázquez, María del Carmen Ramos Ordóñez and Víctor Pavón Vázquez

Introduction

Nowadays, there is a consolidation of educational programmes at the university level that are taught totally or partially in a foreign language, mainly English (Doiz et al., 2013; Macaro et al., 2018; Valcke & Wilkinson, 2017). Today, many universities have reached such a level of expertise that the concern is no longer to create the necessary structure to offer these studies with adequate resources but to ensure that the quality of teaching is not undermined by teaching in a language other than the students' mother tongue (Dafouz, 2018; Dearden, 2014).

For this reason, concern is no longer focused solely on ensuring that these programmes are adequately organised, staffed and resourced but rather on ensuring that the intended learning objectives are achieved (Kremer & Valcke, 2014). The focus has therefore shifted to guaranteeing that what happens in the classroom achieves the desired results (Walenta, 2018). To attain this goal, one of the areas that are receiving the most attention is related to teaching practices (O'Dowd, 2018), above all, everything that refers to the methodological strategies used by the teaching staff (Dimova et al., 2015). It is clear that the pedagogical approach used will determine the results, which is why so much importance is currently given to the methodology to be used by teachers so that students learn in a comfortable and, above all, effective way (Pagèze & Lasagabaster, 2017).

However, a given pedagogical approach cannot be separated from the resources used, of which the utilisation of teaching materials obviously stands out (Tomlinson & Masuhara, 2018). No matter how innovative and potentially effective a particular methodological proposal may be, it will not

DOI: 10.4324/9781003258407-5

be possible to achieve the expected objectives without specially designed materials (Mishan & Timmis, 2015). In the case of teaching highly complex academic content through a foreign language, the importance of having adequate materials at the tertiary level acquires greater value since they are the gateway to knowledge and will regulate the greater or lesser difficulty faced by students (Ávila-López, 2020).

One of the main topics of this chapter is the importance of disciplinary languages. The possession of basic strategies for the comprehension of texts across subject areas and genres, labelled as disciplinary literacy, is different from common language proficiency, which is understood as the global capacity to use the language for the purpose of communicating. The immediate and direct influence that the acquisition of linguistic skills has on the assimilation and manipulation of academic content demands that students get used to the specialised language in the different content areas (Del Pozo, 2017).

The purpose of this chapter is to highlight the importance of language for the construction of knowledge, in particular, the relevance of language specifically linked to subject content. This study offers a series of considerations on how materials should respond to this important dimension of language, concluding with a series of practical recommendations. Finally, we should also clarify that the relevance of designing materials that can cope with the challenges of dealing with disciplinary literacy equally affects content and language integrated learning (CLIL) and English-Medium Instruction (EMI) contexts. Special attention to the language associated with the content material is required in both cases.

Fuelling the Transmission of Content: Attention to Subject-Specific Literacies

One of the hottest debates regarding the suitability of EMI/CLIL is whether it is possible to achieve the same learning objectives compared to studies taught in the learners' mother tongue (Pavón, 2020). Regardless of the linguistic level, some claim that in this type of programme there should be a more accurate consideration of the role of language in learning (Macaro, 2020; Pavón and Ellison, 2021), a focus that should also be reflected in the pedagogy and materials used. On the other hand, for some teachers and experts, attention to language use is secondary; this group believes that, especially in EMI, the only important thing is the content (Airey, 2004; Costa, 2013; Jensen & Thøgersen, 2011). Thus, in a way, they disregard the importance given to the use of language for knowledge construction.

The relevance of language in CLIL/EMI, which is often labelled as academic language and is also known as disciplinary or subject-specific language (Lorenzo & Trujillo, 2017), seems indisputable. The importance of the linguistic dimension for learning has quite often been underestimated (Vollmer, 2006; Roussel et al., 2017). The better the learners' use of specialised language across subjects is, the greater the possibility they acquire a robust use of academic literacies (Airey, 2016; Mancho-Barés & Arnó-Macià, 2017) and a better ability for communication in academic contexts (Björkman, 2011). The reflective and intentional use of this specialised language use consists of a mix of both communicative and discursive planning, both of which can expand learning opportunities (Moore et al., 2014). However, consideration of the relevance of disciplinary languages should not be seen as monolithic, as it may vary according to the area or subject for which the materials are designed. Thus, the type of language required in different subjects will affect the different ways of conceptualising and verbalising knowledge. At the same time, the type of student also affects this consideration, since the characteristics of the learner will also determine the type of language required (Kuteeva & Airey, 2013).

For all the reasons noted earlier, regarding the value of disciplinary languages for the construction of meaning, it is appropriate that relevant linguistic communicative strategies be used (Breeze & Dafouz, 2017; Doiz & Lasagabaster, 2021), and also that teaching be carried out through the use of materials adapted for this purpose (Pimentel & Pavón, 2020). The materials, therefore, must respond to these needs and promote the use of disciplinary languages to make teaching successful.

Principles for the Creation and Adaptation of Materials in EMI/CLIL

The importance of materials in EMI/CLIL classrooms is unquestioned for some authors (Ávila-López, 2020; Pimentel & Pavón, 2020) as these will dramatically influence the desired outcomes (Rose & Galloway, 2019) and are often the most substantial and observable component of pedagogy. We believe it is crucial that materials offer learners "the kind of language in which that knowledge is constructed, evaluated and discussed" (Räsanen & Klaassen, 2004, p. 556).

A reality of EMI/CLIL in university is that using one single textbook is generally not the norm (Dafouz & Núñez, 2009), mainly because of the lack of commercially published textbooks that serve the course goals and scope (Kao & Liao, 2017).

According to Moore and Lorenzo (2007), the lack of commercially available coursebooks/textbooks for EMI/CLIL leads teachers, tutors or lecturers to choose from producing their own materials, using "diluted" materials, or "[adapting] authentic materials in line with their teaching when dealing with the issue of materials" (p. 28). In CLIL/EMI courses in tertiary education, Dafouz and Núñez (2009) reported that materials adaptation was a common methodological strategy, although they did not report on how exactly this adaptation was carried out.

In the case of ESL/EFL, and more recently for EMI/CLIL as well, several authors have developed extensive lists of principles and criteria for the development, selection, adaptation and evaluation of such materials (see Coyle et al., 2010; Guerrini, 2009; Mehisto, 2012; Morton, 2013; Tomlinson, 2016). In relation to EMI and CLIL alone, one of the first attempts to develop such principles was by Guerrini (2009), who stated that materials should be developed on the basis of making subject-specific language salient. This is not to say that subject teachers will have to become language experts; instead, they can be trained to make general academic language salient and explicit for students, and thus it would be ideal if subject-specific language were reflected in materials (Ball, 2018). Following this line of reasoning, Banegas and Manzur (2021) suggest that emphasis should be placed on the kinds of discourses and language use in the subject-specific disciplines and settings students will be required to engage in, and not only on the subsystems of language grammar, lexicon or phonology.

Mehisto's (2012) ten criteria for developing quality materials are an oft-cited set of principles in CLIL, although he has received some criticism for not being CLIL-specific (Banegas, 2018). Some of his principles represent aspects of good pedagogy, and therefore they can be applicable to any type of approach in foreign language teaching and learning; furthermore, only one of them makes explicit reference to language teaching, the rest being meta-disciplinary (Ball, 2018). For Mehisto (2012), materials should systematically foster academic language proficiency. In CLIL research, it is well known that academic language proficiency, or CALP, as opposed to BICS (Basic Interpersonal Communication Strategies), or conversational language (Cummins, 1999), is developed by means of cognitively challenging tasks which are context-reduced.

Characteristics of Effective Materials

More recently, Richards and Pun (2021) have established a classification of EMI instructional materials, offering a review of their characteristics that can be extended to CLIL programmes. According to them, one of the most important characteristics of materials is that they should present authentic content from subject areas to develop academic skills in language programmes. One of the advantages of using authentic texts is that learners can be exposed to the scientific discourses of a specific discipline (i.e. to explanations in science), which is one of the reasons authenticity should also be considered for both text and task selection and creation in EMI/ CLIL (Banegas & Manzur, 2021).

When assessing the effectiveness of CLIL materials, Ball (2018) emphasised that content is three-dimensional and not dichotomous; that is, they cannot be viewed as simply exemplifying the teacher–student relationship. Accessing content involves the presence of a third element, materials. All types of content make up the learning dimensions that can be used as tools and priorities for lesson planning. With this proposal, the notion of content thus includes *language* as content itself. This idea also defends the view that materials should contain support for understanding key ideas and language for solving tasks, and that pedagogic activities and tasks should be geared towards working with spoken and written language skills (Banegas & Manzur, 2021). The idea of language support for task completion is also behind their principle of scaffolding and embedding. The authors claim that the complication stage is the one in which teachers should work with the bulk of CALP because if language that is too complex is used in the orientation stage, learners might get frustrated and lose motivation. In the resolution stage, assessment will take place, and no new concepts should be introduced as this might be counterproductive (Banegas & Manzur, 2021).

Again with regard to specific recommendations for EMI/CLIL, Ávila-López (2020, p. 313) emphasises the use of "authentic language with intellectually demanding activities and creative use of language" and of "pluriliteracies, language (discovery approaches) and cultural awareness". We can see here that he shares with other authors the same concerns for *what* should be included in EMI/CLIL materials: the recommendation of using authentic language (Banegas & Manzur, 2021), the importance of noticing relevant aspects of language by using the so-called discovery approaches, and the development of subject-specific literacies. Herein lies one of the main principles of this chapter, namely, that materials, tasks and activities should promote the work with subject genres and registers or subject-specific literacies, the so-called "pluriliteracies" (Pavón, 2018; Ball, 2018; Meyer et al., 2015). A pluriliteracy model also acknowledges the idea that language is the "primary evidence for learning" (Mohan et al., 2010, p. 221); therefore, learners' successful knowledge acquisition is shown through the appropriate articulation of such knowledge. Furthermore, in CLIL contexts, and we believe also in EMI ones, the cognitive discourse functions or CDFs (Dalton-Puffer, 2013) "lie at the interface between thinking and language" (Meyer et al., 2015, p. 44) as learners must use a set of subject-specific cognitive discourse functions to conceptualise content together with a range of strategies and skills, which are fundamental elements in curriculum learning.

Practical Recommendations to Improve Attention to the Language

Once we have reviewed the criteria that should guide the creation of EMI/CLIL materials, we present a set of practical guidelines concerning attention to the language. It should be noted that the recommendations and suggestions for the creation and adaptation of materials are primarily aimed at language specialist teachers, who would be responsible for implementing them in specific language support courses or using them in counselling sessions and when collaborating with content specialists.

1. Language should be addressed:

    Teachers should focus their attention on presenting subject language and helping their students use it effectively, considering the language as "a means and not an end in itself" (Pimentel & Pavón, 2020, p. 326). Therefore, materials should:

    • inform learners explicitly about the linguistic contents that will be addressed; for example, by including an introductory section in each unit or module where that information is provided in the form of a language box that can be used as a reference section when students are engaged in classroom activities or for the development of tasks. This language box would specify the CDFs and their combinations, evolving into what could be labelled as "complex CDFs" (Breeze & Dafouz, 2017). For instance, in a computing engineering lesson on legislation on cybercrime, students may be asked to define and explain the different types of cybercrime. The language box could be designed as in Table 5.1.

Table 5.1 Model of language box

CDFs	Objective	Linguistic structures	Academic vocabulary
Define/Explain	Define and explain the different types of cybercrime.	– . . . is the use of . . . to cause . . . – An important aspect of cybercrime is . . . – Cybercrime ranges from . . .	blackmail, fraud, spam, attack, infrastructure, cyberterrorism, identity theft, privacy

- include texts, both oral and written, where the "complex CDFs" included in the introductory section are used so that students are exposed to the language they are expected to manage in order to be able to fulfil the tasks and activities addressed in the lessons;
- design tasks which focus on the four linguistic skills (listening, reading, writing and speaking) for the manipulation of content;
- develop academic language by focusing on the grammatical elements (vocabulary and syntax) that verbalise discourse functions.

2. Interaction should be promoted for language use and development:

The successful management of classroom interaction is a requirement for an efficient pedagogy since interaction favours cohesion, leading to comfortability and motivation in a group (Banegas & Manzur, 2021). Therefore, materials should:

- try to maintain students' interest and motivation in participating in classroom interaction by including topics that stimulate their curiosity;
- provide students with the linguistic resources necessary for the negotiation of meaning, for example, with separate lists of expressions;
- promote pair-work and group activities to stimulate interaction;
- propose debates and oral presentations leading to extended questioning.

3. Content and language should be scaffolded:

Scaffolding is a compendium of strategies and resources aimed at providing the necessary help to students so that they can understand and express the content they are working with. Together with the scaffolding of content, which seeks to provide students with the necessary help in understanding concepts and ideas, the scaffolding of language aims at helping them use the linguistic tools necessary for the elaboration and transmission of meaning. This language scaffolding is linked to focus on language, which was described in the first recommendation. Therefore, materials should:

- provide activities highlighting the linguistic elements that help the expression of meaning;

- extensively use visual aids such as graphs, diagrams, tables and mind maps;
- offer activities in which the content is presented in different ways, for example, by using videos and reading material on the same topic;
- make students reformulate content through various formats (for example, an interview could become a narration, or a written description could be changed to an oral argumentation).

4. Language and content should be assessed:

Assessment is necessary to know if the objectives have been achieved in both their summative and formative nature. It is used to collaborate with the teaching process itself and for its diagnostic dimension as a tool to determine the characteristics of the teaching (Mohan et al., 2010). Teachers would do well to incorporate activities that provide them with detailed and varied information on students' progress. Therefore, materials should:

- present activities that are connected to the assessment criteria and are clearly identified;
- present assessment tools of a formal (tests) and informal nature (diaries, self-assessment, portfolios, assessments of projects, etc.);
- use accessible language in the activities intended to be used for assessment so that students understand how the activities should be addressed using the cognitive processes or CDFs practiced in the lessons;
- include activities that promote self-assessment and self-reflection on the part of the students.

5. A Task-based Learning approach should be used:

The use of tasks has a direct impact on students' communicative competence, cognitive development and motivation as they involve attention to meaning and real language use, which is achieved by means of all linguistic skills and the activation of different cognitive processes. Making students carry out meaningful activities with the objective of developing a relevant product will ensure that language and content are correctly integrated. Materials should:

- guarantee that students become the main actors in the tasks to be performed, that task fulfilment is sufficiently motivating and demanding, and that the final product is relevant to the learning objectives;

- promote content understanding and information access, and allow students to formulate acquired knowledge by means of activities that are linked with previous knowledge;
- be adapted to the students' diversified linguistic competences by offering different degrees of task completion;
- promote interdisciplinary and cross-curricular material to benefit from the thematic connection with other disciplines.

6. A genre-based pedagogy should be implemented:

   This approach generally focuses on the production of written texts. However, it could also be used for guiding the production of oral texts in EMI/CLIL contexts (Morton, 2010). This pedagogy is useful in approaching the discourse structure intrinsic to texts in different subjects, and its benefits at different educational levels are well-documented (Dafouz & Núñez, 2009). One way to explicitly develop academic language is to focus on the genres that are typical of the subjects in which they appear. Focusing on the different genres of content subjects keeps the teacher informed about the levels of linguistic competence in the foreign language and facilitates the assessment of learning. Similarly, planning and working specifically with the language functions related to the genre types also helps to consolidate communication strategies (Morton, 2020).

Conclusion

This chapter has addressed one key element for the success of EMI/CLIL programmes at tertiary level: the design of materials, specifically, the presence and treatment of disciplinary language in those teaching materials. As we have seen, some authors claim that command of the language of instruction by students is not enough to guarantee good results in EMI/CLIL courses (Breeze & Dafouz, 2017; Doiz & Lasagabaster, 2021). Apart from properly planning university programmes and training teachers in methodologies which ease the teaching of content through a foreign language, having materials specifically designed for that purpose is crucial. In line with different experts' recommendations (Banegas & Manzur, 2021; Meyer et al., 2015; Morton, 2010, 2020), we propose the design of teaching materials which follow a set of practical guidelines for the treatment of the disciplinary language in EMI/CLIL: the explicit treatment of language necessary to develop cognitive processes, the promotion of interaction, language and content scaffolding and assessment, the design of real and demanding tasks which enhance motivation and participation, and the use of the textual genres, both oral and written, characteristic of the area of expertise. If what

EMI/CLIL students need to prove is their command of the competences listed in the programmes they are enrolled in, the only means to accomplish that is by academic literacy (Airey, 2016; Kuteeva & Airey, 2013). Therefore, there is no doubt that the way in which language is used must be present in the teaching practices, which involves materials purposefully designed that explicitly state the adequate use of CDFs and their linguistic structures and vocabulary necessary for the domain of content, the achievement of objectives, and, lastly, competence in the field (Mancho-Barés & Arnó-Macià, 2017; Meyer & Coyle, 2017).

Nevertheless, future studies should involve an in-depth evaluation and analysis of these practical recommendations for developing *quality* materials in important areas of materials input, different types of pedagogic tasks, output promotion, scaffolding, and any other aspect relevant for students considering EMI/CLIL-specific learning-teaching contexts. Moreover, we believe that providing a standardised framework for EMI materials could ease the lecturers' task, reduce anxiety and make the process of materials creation less time-consuming.

References

Airey, J. (2004). Can you teach it in English? Aspects of the language choice debate in Swedish higher education. In R. Wilkinson (Ed.), *Integrating content and language. Meeting the challenge of a multilingual higher education* (pp. 97–108). Maastricht University.

Airey, J. (2016). CLIL and EAP (Content and language integrated learning and English for academic purposes). In K. Hyland & P. Shaw (Eds.), *Routledge handbook of English for academic purposes* (pp. 71–83). Routledge.

Ávila-López, J. (2020). Materials development. A constituent element of teacher training for EMI in higher education. In M. M. Sánchez-Pérez (Ed.), *Teacher training for English-medium instruction in higher education* (pp. 298–319). IGI Global.

Ball, P. (2018). Innovations and challenges in CLIL materials design. *Theory Into Practice, 57*(3), 222–231.

Banegas, D. L. (2018). Evaluating language and content in coursebooks. In M. Azarnoosh, M. Zeraatpishe, A. Faravani, & H. R. Kargozari (Eds.), *Issues in coursebook evaluation* (pp. 21–29). Brill.

Banegas, D. L., & Manzur, G. (2021). EMI materials in online initial English language teacher education. In D. Lasagabaster & A. Doiz (Eds.), *Language use in English-medium instruction at university* (pp. 100–125). Routledge.

Björkman, B. (2011). Pragmatic strategies in English as an academic lingua franca: Ways of achieving communicative effectiveness? *Journal of Pragmatics, 43*(4), 950–964.

Breeze, R., & Dafouz, E. (2017). Constructing complex cognitive discourse functions in higher education. An exploratory study of exam answers in Spanish- and English-medium instruction settings. *System, 70,* 81–91.

Costa, F. (2013). Dealing with the language aspect? Personally no. Content lecturers' views of teaching through English in an ICLHE context. In S. Breidbach & B. Viebrock (Eds.), *Content and language integrated learning in Europe* (pp. 117–127). Peter Lang.

Coyle, D., Hood, P., & Marsh, D. (2010). *CLIL: Content and language integrated learning*. Cambridge University Press.

Cummins, J. (1999). *BICS and CALP: Clarifying the distinction* (Report No. ED438551) (pp. 2–7). US Department of Education ERIC.

Dafouz, E. (2018). English-medium instruction and teacher education programmes in higher education: Ideological forces and imagined identities at work. *International Journal of Bilingual Education and Bilingualism, 21*(5), 540–552.

Dafouz, E., & Núñez, B. (2009). CLIL in higher education: Devising a new learning landscape. In E. Dafouz & M. C. Guerrini (Eds.), *CLIL across educational levels: Experiences from primary, secondary and tertiary contexts* (pp. 101–112). Santillana Educación S.L.-Richmond Publishing.

Dalton-Puffer, C. (2013). A construct of cognitive discourse functions for conceptualising content-language integration in CLIL and multilingual education. *European Journal of Applied Linguistics, 1*(2), 216–253.

Dearden, J. (2014). *English as a medium of instruction: A growing phenomenon*. British Council.

Del Pozo, M. A. (2017). Academic discourse in English medium instruction contexts: A look at teacher explanations. *EPIC Language and Linguistics, 2*, 112–118.

Dimova, S., Hultgren, A. K., & Jensen, C. (Eds.). (2015). English-medium instruction in European higher education. In *Language and social life* (p. 4). De Gruyter Mouton.

Doiz, A., & Lasagabaster, D. (2021). An analysis of the use of cognitive discourse functions in English-medium history teaching at university. *System, 62*, 58–69.

Doiz, A., Lasagabaster, D., & Sierra, J. M. (Eds.). (2013). *English-medium instruction at universities: Global challenges*. Multilingual Matters.

Guerrini, M. (2009). CLIL materials as scaffolds to learning. In D. Marsh, P. Mehisto, D. Wolff, R. Aliaga, T. Asikainen, M. Frigols-Martin, S. Hughes, & G. Langé (Eds.), *CLIL practice: Perspectives from the field* (pp. 74–84). Universidad de Jyväskylä.

Jensen, C., & Thøgersen, J. (2011). Danish university lecturers' attitudes towards English as the medium of instruction. *Ibérica, 22*, 13–34.

Kao, S. M., & Liao, H. T. (2017). Developing glocalized materials for EMI courses in the humanities. In *English as a medium of instruction in higher education* (pp. 147–162). Springer.

Kremer, M., & Valcke, J. (2014). Teaching and learning in English in higher education: A literature review. In *EDULEARN 14 proceedings* (pp. 1430–1441). IATED.

Kuteeva, M., & Airey, J. (2013). Disciplinary differences in the use of English in higher education: Reflections on recent policy developments. *Higher Education, 67*(5), 1–18.

Lorenzo, F., & Trujillo, F. (2017). Languages of schooling in European policymaking: Present state and future outcomes. *European Journal of Applied Linguistics, 5*(2), 177–197.

Macaro, E. (2020). Exploring the role of language in English medium instruction, *International Journal of Bilingual Education and Bilingualism, 23*(3), 263–276.

Macaro, E., Curle, S., Pun, J., An, J., & Dearden, J. (2018). A systematic review of English medium instruction in higher education. *Language Teaching, 51*(1), 36–76.

Mancho-Barés, G., & Arnó-Macià, E. (2017). EMI lecturer training programmes and academic literacies: A critical insight from ESP. *ESP Today, 5*(2), 266–290.

Mehisto, P. (2012). Criteria for producing CLIL learning materials. *Encuentro, 21*, 15–33.

Meyer, O., & Coyle, D. (2017). Pluriliteracies teaching for learning: Conceptualizing progression for deeper learning in literacies development. *European Journal of Applied Linguistics, 5*(2), 199–222.

Meyer, O., Coyle, D., Halbach, A., Schuck, K., & Ting, T. (2015). A pluriliteracies approach to content and language integrated learning – mapping learner progressions in knowledge construction and meaning-making. *Language, Culture and Curriculum, 28*(1), 41–57.

Mishan, F., & Timmis, I. (2015). *Materials development for TESOL*. Edinburgh University Press.

Mohan, B., Leung, C., & Slater, T. (2010). Assessing language and content: A functional perspective. In A. Paran & L. Sercu (Eds.), *Testing the untestable in language education* (pp. 217–240). Multilingual Matters.

Moore, P., & Lorenzo, F. (2007). Adapting authentic materials for CLIL classrooms: An empirical study. *VIEWZ: Vienna English Working Papers, 16*(3), 28–35.

Moore, P., Márquez, M., & Gutiérrez, V. (2014). La optimización del discurso del aula en el aprendizaje integrado de contenidos y lengua [The optimization of classroom discourse in integrated learning of content and language]. *Magazin/Extra, 1*, 44–49.

Morton, T. (2010). Using a genre-based approach to integrating content and language in CLIL. In C. Dalton-Puffer, T. Nikula, & U. Smit (Eds.), *Language use and language learning in CLIL classrooms* (pp. 81–104). John Benjamins.

Morton, T. (2013). Critically evaluating materials for CLIL: Practitioners' practices and perspectives. In J. Gray (Ed.), *Critical perspectives on language teaching materials* (pp. 111–136). Springer.

Morton, T. (2020). Cognitive discourse functions: A bridge between content, literacy and language for teaching and assessment in CLIL. *CLIL Journal of Innovation and Research in Plurilingual and Pluricultural Education, 3*(1), 7–17.

O'Dowd, R. (2018). The training and accreditation of teachers for English medium instruction: An overview of practice in European universities. *International Journal of Bilingual Education and Bilingualism, 21*, 553–563.

Pagèze, J., & Lasagabaster, D. (2017). Teacher development for teaching and learning in English in a French higher education context. *L'analisi linguistica e letteraria, XXV*, 289–311.

Pavón, V. (2018). Innovations and challenges in CLIL research: Exploring the development of subject specific literacies. *Theory into Practice, 57*(3), 204–211.

Pavón, V. (2020). The role of languages in the internationalisation of higher education: Institutional challenges. In R. Rubio & D. Coyle (Eds.), *Quality of bilingual programmes in higher education* (pp. 96–114). Multilingual Matters.

Pavón, V., & Ellison, M. (2021). Implementing EMI in higher education: Language use, language research and professional development. In D. Lasagabaster & A. Doiz (Eds.), *Language use in English-medium instruction at university international perspectives on teacher practice* (pp. 193–212). Routledge.

Pimentel, C., & Pavón, V. (2020). The pedagogical dimension and the use of materials in English-taught programs in higher education. In M. M. Sánchez-Pérez (Ed.), *Teacher training for English-medium instruction in higher education* (pp. 320–339). IGI Global.

Räsanen, A., & Klaassen, R. G. (2004). Academic competences in a multilingual learning environment. In R. Wilkinson (Ed.), *Integrating content and language: Meeting the challenge of a multilingual higher education* (pp. 565–570). Universitaire Pers Maastricht.

Richards, J. C., & Pun, J. (2021). A typology of English-medium instruction. *RELC Journal, 1*, 25.

Rose, H., & Galloway, N. (2019). *Global Englishes for language teaching*. Cambridge University Press.

Roussel, S., Joulia, D., Tricot, A., & Sweller, J. (2017). Learning subject content through a foreign language should not ignore human cognitive structure: A cognitive load theory approach. *Learning and Instruction, 52*, 69–79.

Tomlinson, B. (2016). Achieving a match between SLA theory and materials development. In B. Tomlinson (Ed.), *SLA research and materials development for language learning* (pp. 3–22). Routledge.

Tomlinson, B., & Masuhara, H. (2018). *The complete guide to the theory and practice of materials development for language learning*. John Wiley & Sons.

Valcke, J., & Wilkinson, R. (Eds.). (2017). *Integrating content and language in higher education: Perspectives and professional practice*. Peter Lang.

Vollmer, H. (2006). *Languages across the curriculum*. Council of Europe.

Walenta, M. (2018). Balancing linguistic and extra-linguistic gains in CLIL: A case for content-based structured input. *International Journal of Bilingual Education and Bilingualism, 21*(5), 578–590.

6 EMI With a Twist

A Multimodal Analysis of Student–Teacher Agency in the Classroom

Monica Clua[1] and Natalia Evnitskaya

Introduction

The university lecture is generally considered an oral tradition (Arminen, 2017; Malavska, 2016) and hence questions have been raised by teachers and students about the effectiveness of English as a medium of instruction when it is nobody's L1 (Jenkins, 2011). Yet, a sociocultural multimodal prism (for instance, see Mondada, 2016) reveals the university lecture, seen as a spoken genre (Malavska, 2016) and as an encounter (Goffman, 1981), to be an interaction. Based on the premise that reciprocal discourse mediates learning (Escobar Urmeneta & Walsh, 2017), sociocultural perspectives suggest that the student-as-novice, and not just the teacher-as-expert, co-constructs and regulates the space for learning (Pekarek Doehler, 2002). That the teacher has epistemic authority through their content knowledge expertise is a social given (Hofstede, 1986). However, EMI might challenge the traditional dichotomy of teacher-as-expert versus student-as-novice as mutually exclusive roles. For instance, a complex epistemic situation may arise should students have *higher* general English language proficiency than the lecturer. Would the lecturer's epistemic status and authority be undermined? How would students and teachers orient towards each other under these circumstances? These questions call for socio-interactional methodologies (see Mori, 2004) to understand socialisation processes in the EMI context, in this case, how institutional identities are constructed *through and for* classroom interaction. There is a paucity of interactional research on EMI (Matsumoto & Canagarajah, 2020) and no study to our knowledge has investigated the teacher–student relationship in higher education through such a lens.

Conceptual Framework

Institutional interactions are asymmetrical and driven by procedural goals (Drew & Heritage, 1992), for instance, *doing* being a teacher is enacted

DOI: 10.4324/9781003258407-6

differently from *doing* being a student (Sacks, 1984). These are recognised as two different *activity types* as conventionalised boundaries, or constraints, delineate each role, and where "having a grasp of the meaning of utterances involves knowing the nature of the activity in which the utterances play a role" (Levinson, 1992, p. 66). Hence, an activity type provides context for meaning-making in social interaction. In the classroom, boundaries are visible in spatial arrangements, speakership rights, length of speaking turns and turn content (Sacks et al., 1974), where a breach of any such conventions would reveal the constraints at play.

Hence, *constraints* act on the *scope* of one's agentive capacity (Latour, 2005). Broadly speaking, *agency* is "the sociocultural mediated capacity to act" (Ahearn, 2001, p. 112). To illustrate, how a question might be issued, received and responded to in the classroom is contingent on and displays one's institutional position, in this case, whether one is a teacher or a student (Depperman, 2013). Moreover, *agentive actions* are driven by *intentionality* (Gallagher & Zahavi, 2012), the goal-directed orientation in action; "[J]ust as my intentions are explicit in my actions, I understand your intentions to be explicit in yours. Intentions are not hidden in the mind but expressed in [corporeal] behaviour" (idem, p. 167). Altogether, *agentive actions* are those that bear on the unfolding of an activity in a transformative and decisive capacity (Klemenčič, 2017).

In light of the above, specific pedagogical and institutional objectives characterise teacher and student roles as complementary one to the other (Hofstede, 1986), whereby teachers teach so that learners can learn (Seedhouse, 2004). As such, the teacher-fronted arrangement in the classroom is one *embodied* display of the teacher's epistemic status and authority (Lim et al., 2012). Meanwhile, in discourse, roles are visible in the distribution and length of speaking turns (Sacks et al., 1974), in turn allocation (Evnitskaya & Berger, 2017) and in turn content (Drew & Heritage, 1992), where teacher talk is expected to display expert stances, while student talk would indicate novice status (Stivers et al., 2011). These positions are generally uncontested because they form the *Habitus* (Bourdieu, 1977a) of the teacher–student relationship, in other words, the "[I]nternalised structures, schemes of perception, conception, and embodiment of these, common to all members of the same group or class" (p. 86).

However, the EMI context may present unique challenges to this relationship if we consider the epistemic domains particular to EMI. Due to the widespread use of English in academia, EMI teachers may have greater mastery of professional discourses in English than they do of general English. Conversely, international and even domestic students might possess high competence in general English, but not in subject matter discourse in any language (Macaro, 2018). Hence, *specific disciplinary* discourse knowledge in English is one epistemic domain, while *general* English knowledge is another (Airey & Linder, 2009). Heritage (2012, p. 4) suggests using the symbols $K+$ and $K-$ to denote the knowledge status between individuals, or groups, in a given domain, where $K+$ means "more knowledgeable" and $K-$ refers to "less knowledgeable". From an interactional perspective, the $K+/K-$ gradient is one driver in negotiating *shared understanding* (see, e.g. Duranti, 2010) and *knowledge progression* (Balaman & Sert, 2017).

And here comes the *twist*. Given that a (teacher's) content $K+$ status suggests epistemic authority, how might students who are linguistically $K+$, that is, possess higher *general English language* knowledge, respond to the input of a linguistically $K-$ teacher? Students' displays of linguistic $K+$ could *undermine* the EMI teacher's epistemic authority and status, which could lead to a transgression of traditional roles and altered power relations (Bourdieu, 1977b). Moreover, a student who initiates a (language-related) repair sequence could be perceived as committing "epistemic trespassing" (Stivers et al., 2011, p. 19). Pekarek Doehler (2002) casts a hopeful and constructive light on this supposedly tense situation:

> [D]ialogue as well as collaborative problem-solving imply not simply the roles of knower versus not-knower, but for instance, the ones of thematic guide versus follower, of questioner and respondent, of co-constructor of activities and so on. In the dynamic course of interaction, *roles mingle, their boundaries dissolve* and they give place to a reciprocal shaping of mediational processes.
>
> (pp. 25–26, italics ours)

Thus, the objectives of this chapter are twofold:

1. To demonstrate the contribution that a qualitative, micro-analytic, socio-interactional emic approach can make to understand the EMI context.
2. To explore one particular phenomenon through the study of a single case of student–teacher agency in light of institutional roles and constraints in the EMI classroom. Specifically, how a *linguistically $K+$/content $K-$ student* orients her agentive actions to the input of a *linguistically $K-$/content $K+$ teacher*.

Methodological Framework

Participants

The sequence examined in this chapter belongs to a corpus of EMI classroom data extensively analysed in Clua Serrano[1] (2021) and comes from a

45-minute lesson on Dental Materials given to second-year international Dentistry students in a private Catalan university in Barcelona, Spain. According to official admission records, the students' level of general English language proficiency was mostly C1 (CEFR). The lecturer (DM) is an experienced teacher of Dental Materials in Spanish and Catalan, and it was her second year teaching this subject in English. Her English language proficiency at the time of data collection was below B2 (CEFR). Furthermore, she failed the official exam *Certificat de Llengües de les Universitats de Catalunya* (CLUC-EMI, Language Certificate issued by Catalan universities) used to certify a lecturer's capacity to teach subject matter in English and required by many Catalan universities. Moreover, DM rarely asks students questions about the subject matter to evaluate their knowledge status, however, the practices revealed in the data show this teacher's classroom to be a co-constructed epistemically progressive environment as she fosters participation by welcoming students' interjections. The data presented herein focuses on the interaction between one student (ST) and DM.

Data Treatment and Analytical Tools

Interactional studies rely on audiovisual recordings to produce fine-grained analyses of how social actions sequentially emerge and evolve through interaction. Linking video analysis software, Transana™ (Basic version 3.30-Mac), was used to facilitate repeated listening and viewing of the recordings, from which transcripts of the talk were produced using standard Conversation Analysis conventions (Jefferson, 1984; see also Bezemer & Mavers, 2011) to highlight prosodic features of speech (see Appendix 1). Under the premise that meaning-making is not exclusively bound by words (see Goffman, 1981; Goodwin, 2007), video grabs showing crucial shifts in gaze, gesture and spatial conduct are presented alongside the transcript (Norris, 2004). This study intends to shine a light on the *multimodal* dynamics of discourse co-construction (see Hazel, 2014) in student–teacher agentive actions and displays of epistemic status.

To access an emic perspective, that is, the participants' viewpoint, *Conversation Analysis* (CA), originating in ethnomethodology and with roots in phenomenology, provides researchers with a toolkit for fine-grained, turn-by-turn sequential analysis of emerging social actions (e.g. requesting, mitigating or apologising) (Schegloff, 2007). To borrow an analogy from Heritage and Maynard (2006), it is the sequence and position of words and actions in a given context that gives rise to a specific meaning, in the same way that the sequence and position of base nucleotides on a strand of DNA, and not simply their relative proportions, give rise to the expression of biological characteristics. Further insight into interactional dynamics is provided by our common-sense knowledge of social categories such as "teacher" or "mother" (Sacks, 1992). Thus, to address the issue of how *social categories* can *mediate* interactions, *Membership Categorisation Analysis* (Housley & Fitzgerald, 2015; Sacks, 1992) and the notion of *Positioning* (Depperman, 2013) can be applied to identify how participants orient to their social category and to that of the other in a certain social system (Latour, 2005). In this study, such a laminated lens allowed us to reveal turn-by-turn-generated identities *in* interaction and *for* interaction (Antaki et al., 1996) in the EMI classroom.

Single Case Analyses

Whilst in CA a collection of cases highlights the recurrence of a particular behaviour, the observations generated by a single case underscore past work on a range of phenomena which is then brought to bear on a single sequence (Mori, 2004; Yin, 2009). In other words, past CA work can illuminate an interactional trajectory and its outcome. For instance, the single case analysis by Whalen et al. (1988, cited in Mori, 2004) reveals how the mitigated speech of a caller to the emergency services led to the delayed arrival of an ambulance and the subsequent death of the patient. Another well-known example is Goodwin's (1995) multimodal CA analysis of a girls' game of hopscotch, which provided evidence to contest the popular idea that girls' play lacked intellectual complexity. Therefore, single cases are of interest in and of themselves, where the case presented in this chapter is motivated by pedagogical concerns in EMI.

Data Analysis and Findings

The sequence examined here shows the end of DM's explanation of the moulding properties of alginate, a material used to make dental impressions, when a student (ST) interjects requesting clarification. In this classroom, what follows are the moves DM and ST make to accomplish shared understanding whilst orienting to their institutional roles. This single sequence was broken down into six shorter excerpts to facilitate analysis and reading. Superscript numbers in the transcript mark points of actions.

Excerpt 6.1: DM is concluding her explanation of the relationship between the alginate's moulding capacity, "deformation", and its strength, "resistance to tear" (lines 1–2, figures 1 and 2) where she depicts "deformation" by making a claw-like shape with her right hand (figure 1). She pronounces "tear" as /tir/, a significant detail which we revisit later. Then in line 2, while stating that the moulding and tearing properties are closely related, her hands engage in an inversely rotating gesture (figure 2), which

Excerpt 6.1

Line	Speaker/Transcript	Figures
1	DM: the [1]deformation the permanent deformation and the resistance to /tir/	
2	are very [2]close (1.0) one to each other↓ (0.4) ok↑	

Excerpt 6.2

Line	Speaker/Transcript	Figures
3	ST: [4]wait so you mea:n	
4	more [5]water (0.7) makes it er more likely [6]to tear↑	

may *visually* communicate an inverse relationship between the two stated properties. DM signals the end of this explanation with falling intonation, a short pause and a rising "ok" (line 2).

Excerpt 6.2: In line 3, ST interjects with "wait" whilst leaning forward and extending her hand in a "halt" gesture (figure 3), her micro pause producing a summoning effect (Goodwin & Goodwin, 2004) on DM (figure 4). Once DM's attention is visually secured, ST continues "so you mea:n" (line 3), indexing communication trouble and the initiation of a repair sequence (Schegloff, 2007). ST's arm remains extended, allowing her to retain speakership (Clua Serrano, 2021), as she gestures through line 4 (see figures 5 and 6). As she presents her understanding of water-to-powder ratio for evaluation (line 4), her head is subtly cocked to the side, displaying deference to DM (see Straus, 1952). ST's agentive move orients to DM's content $K+$ status, in turn embodying her content $K-$ status and *learner* category.

Excerpt 6.3: The teacher responds with "more water *what*?" (line 5), which either indexes her mishearing, or her linguistic $K-$ status. DM positions herself closer to ST, thereby creating a focused space (see figure 15 in Excerpt 6.4). ST proceeds to unpack the question (lines 6–10). In line 6, ST summons attention to her turn with "so". "more" is emphasised by prolonging the vowel sound. Simultaneously, her left-hand palm up is directed at DM (figure 7). DM's "yes" (line 7) sets up ST's reformulation of "more water" (line 6) as "more concentration of water" in line 8, a more scientific rendering. Figures 8 and 9 show how ST depicts "concentration"; she *adds* her right hand on top of her left. DM inserts a validating "yes" (line 9) in ST's stream of talk, so in line 10 ST further extends line 8 to "water to powder mixture". Figures 10 and 11 show her left hand, representing "water", is placed on her right hand, the "powder". This excerpt shows ST enacting a teaching-like sequence that is oriented to an assumed linguistic, not content, $K-$ status of DM.

Excerpt 6.4: Lines 11 and 12 expose ST's core inquiry. As she prolongs the sound on "more", she extends her hands before her (figure 12), whereas on "less", she retracts them (figure 13), in a manner highlighting and visually depicting "more" and "less". On "t'tear" (line 13), ST momentarily points to the slide (figure 14/15), then immediately tucks her hands close to her body (figure 16), thereby relinquishing speakership.

Thus far, we can argue that ST's question reformulation (lines 6–12) displayed a clear orientation to DM's linguistic $K-$ status *and* content $K+$ status. ST's original question included the terms "likely" and "tear", neither Latinate cognates. Moreover, ST's non-rhotic British pronunciation of "tear" (rhyming with non-rhotic "air") stood in contrast to DM's rhotic pronunciation /tir/ (line 2). ST seems to intuit that "likely" and "tear" are possible

Excerpt 6.3

Line	Speaker/ Transcript	Figures
5	**DM**: more water what↑	
6	**ST**: so mo:re ⁷water	
7	**DM**: y[es	
8	**ST**: [more ⁸concentration⁹ of water=	
9	**DM**: =yes=	
10	**ST**: = ¹⁰water to ¹¹powder mixture(.)	

sources of trouble, thus she replaces "likely" with "resistant" (line 12), and on "tear" she points and directs her gaze to the keyword on the slide (figure 14/15). Gaze and pointing are deictic signals (Kidwell, 2013), so DM responds by turning to the slide (figure 16).

Switching from "likely" to "resistant" aligns ST with DM's linguistic *K-* status, moreover, ST inadvertently takes up an element of subject matter discourse. Hence, *ST's language* is shaped by DM's discourse and slide contents. Nevertheless, slide contents belong to the teacher's domain; when ST interacts with and incorporates slide contents into her talk, she seems aware of having trespassed the teacher–student boundary by her prompt *embodied* withdrawal. So, lines 6–10 show ST positioned as *teacher*-learner, a twist in conventional arrangements, whereas lines 11–12 show ST oriented back to *learner*-teacher as she visually and verbally presents her question

Excerpt 6.4

Line	Speaker/Transcript	Figures
11	would make it(.)¹²mo:re	
12	or ¹³less resistant(.)¹⁴/¹⁵ t'tear	
	(3.0)¹⁶	

Excerpt 6.5

Line	Speaker/Transcript	Figure
13	**DM**: °it's less resistant↓°	
14	**ST**: ¹⁷less↑ resistant	

to DM for evaluation. Although membership categories (teacher/student) become somewhat blurred in the interaction, ST's agentive action is driven by her content *K-* status, hence she ultimately positions herself in the learner role and DM in the teacher role in terms of subject matter knowledge.

Excerpt 6.5: After a three-second pause, DM answers that the mixture is *less* resistant to tear (line 13), in a quieter voice, which may indicate uncertainty. ST responds with a mildly emphatic "<u>less</u> resistant?" (line 14). ST may have expected "more" to be the answer (see line 11). However, she *mitigates* this utterance through embodied conduct; she peers up at DM from a slightly lowered head (compare with a student in the foreground), whilst keeping her hands close to her body (figure 17). Here, ST again exerts her agentive capacity in *doing* questioning (Sacks, 1984) of DM's response. ST orients to DM's responsibility for $K+$ field knowledge (Heritage, 2012), *yet* she mitigates her actions through corporeal behaviour, ensuring respective membership categories are kept stable.

Excerpt 6.6: In line 15, DM initially responds with "no", thereby aligning with ST's casting of doubt. However, after a two-second pause, she switches

Excerpt 6.6

Line	Speaker/Transcript	Figures
15	**DM**: no (2.0) [18]yes because(.)I said	
16	if you [19]change the if you:: put less water	
17	you increase the [20]<u>strength</u>	

(*Continued*)

76 *Monica Clua and Natalia Evnitskaya*

Excerpt 6.6 (Continued)

Line	Speaker/Transcript	Figures
18	and the [21]resistance	
19	to [22]°/tier/°	
20	ST: yeah↑	

her answer (line 15), signalling her shift in stance with an "authoritative" pointing gesture (figure 18). Although line 16 presents a false start, DM sweeps her "authoritative" pointing finger to the slide to *highlight* the key terms in her explanation sequence, as seen in lines 16–19, through which she creates visual continuity of her institutional authority and reclaims her expert status with a multimodal display of subject matter knowledge.

By this point, DM has been exposed to a British pronunciation of "tear" twice (lines 4 and 12), such that her own pronunciation of this term in line 19 is uttered as /tier/. Interestingly, when she points and utters "tier", her voice becomes quieter (line 19), thereby momentarily embodying an uncertain learner.[2] Finally, after an epistemically complex interaction, in line 20, ST responds affirmatively with "yeah!" to the input of DM, a linguistically $K-$/content $K+$ teacher.

Discussion and Concluding Remarks

The first objective of this study was to demonstrate how a qualitative, micro-analytic, interactional and emic approach, through a combination of tools from multimodal Conversation Analysis, Membership Categorisation

Analysis, and Positioning, can contribute to and deepen our understanding of the EMI context. The second aim was to examine student–teacher agency in terms of institutional roles and constraints in such educational settings, specifically how linguistically $K+$/content $K-$ students orient their agentive actions to the input of a linguistically $K-$/content $K+$ teacher.

The findings generated by a single case can allow for a series of observations. In terms of student agency, the sequence examined showcases an unusual but well-established dynamic that affords students opportunities to shape the unfolding of the class. For instance, ST oriented to the teacher's linguistic and content competence through the *initiation* of a repair sequence. Unconventional uses of English by DM (line 2 is an example of instances identified in the data corpus) did not elicit repair sequences from any student, instead they seemed to apply the *let it pass* principle, understood as the normalisation of ELF within a paradigm of pragmatic use (Firth, 1996). This allows us to hypothesise that students' interjections occur when *epistemic progression* is at stake.

In orienting to DM's *linguistic $K-$* status, ST redesigned her question and deployed gestures to further relieve the task of listening and comprehension as she enacted the combination of the substances and quantifiers, and pointed to the relevant term. In short, ST temporarily positioned herself in a teacher role to align with DM's linguistic $K-$ in order to *access* DM's content expertise. Nevertheless, ST consistently oriented to DM's *epistemic $K+$* status and membership category by *mitigating* her actions through *embodied* means, for instance, in her upward gaze from a slightly lowered head, and retraction of her hands into her personal space. In other words, ST's demeanour bore no signs of a power shift in favour of her linguistic $K+$. Nonetheless, DM *reclaimed* her epistemic authority at the end of the sequence. The interaction overall led to the co-construction of subject matter discourse, in which both the teacher *and* the student participated in instructional sequences and learning opportunities. These findings are consistent across the broader data corpus (Clua Serrano, 2021).

Yet, what can this single case contribute to understanding the EMI context? Firstly, that teachers' high general English proficiency might be ideal, but not absolutely fundamental in the EMI classroom (see Allan & Bradbeer, 2019). Creating an educational experience is not just a matter of teachers' linguistic competence but of *facilitating interaction with students*. Concretely, the sequence illustrated how a linguistic $K+/-$ gradient and trouble in understanding can create opportunities for student–teacher interaction. Furthermore, it illustrated the central roles of embodied actions in the construction of knowledge, epistemic status and institutional roles. This sociocultural perspective places EMI teachers within an empowering "can do" paradigm from which they can encourage and harness students' agentive actions.

Notes

1 "M. Clua" and "M. Clua Serrano" (PhD dissertation reference) are the same author.
2 In a follow-up data session with the researcher, DM agreed with this interpretation, reporting she is always trying to learn from the students.

References

Ahearn, L. M. (2001). Language and agency. *Annual Review of Anthropology*, *30*(1), 109–137.
Airey, J., & Linder, C. (2009). A disciplinary discourse perspective on university science learning: Achieving fluency in a critical constellation of modes. *Journal of Research in Science Teaching: The Official Journal of the National Association for Research in Science Teaching*, *46*(1), 27–49.
Allan, W., & Bradbeer, M. (2019, April 4). *The role of serial and one-off observations in EMI lecturer development*. Paper presentation, EMI Practices in Europe, University of Copenhagen.
Antaki, C., Condor, S., & Levine, M. (1996). Social identities in talk: Speakers' own orientations. *British Journal of Social Psychology*, *35*(4), 473–492. doi:10.1111/j.2044-8309.1996.tb01109.x
Arminen, I. (2017). Classrooms and the transmission of knowledge and expertise. In I. Arminen (Ed.), *Institutional interaction* (pp. 112–134). Routledge.
Balaman, U., & Sert, O. (2017). The coordination of online L2 interaction and orientations to task interface for epistemic progression. *Journal of Pragmatics*, *115*, 115–129.
Bezemer, J., & Mavers, D. (2011). Multimodal transcription as academic practice: A social semiotic perspective. *International Journal of Social Research Methodology*, *14*(3), 191–206.
Bourdieu, P. (1977a). *Outline of a theory of practice*. Cambridge University Press.
Bourdieu, P. (1977b). The economics of linguistic exchanges. *Social Science Information*, *16*(6), 645–668. doi:10.1177/053901847701600601
Clua Serrano, M. (2021). *Can you see what I mean? A multimodal approach to interactional competence in English-medium instruction* (Doctoral dissertation, Universitat Internacional de Catalunya). Tesis Doctorals en Xarxa (tdx.cat).
Deppermann, A. (2013). How to get a grip on identities-in-interaction: (What) does 'positioning' offer more than 'membership categorization'? Evidence from a mock story. *Narrative Inquiry*, *23*(1), 62–88.
Drew, P., & Heritage, J. (1992). Analyzing talk at work: An introduction. In P. Drew & J. Heritage (Eds.), *Talk at work* (1st ed., pp. 3–65). Cambridge University Press.
Duranti, A. (2010). Husserl, intersubjectivity and anthropology. *Anthropological Theory*, *10*(1–2), 16–35.
Escobar Urmeneta, C., & Walsh, S. (2017). Classroom interactional competence in content and language integrated learning. In A. Llinares & T. Morton (Eds.), *Applied linguistics perspectives on CLIL* (pp. 183–201). John Benjamins.

Evnitskaya, N., & Berger, E. (2017). Learners' multimodal displays of willingness to participate in classroom interaction in the L2 and CLIL contexts. *Classroom Discourse*, *8*(1), 71–94.

Firth, A. (1996). The discursive accomplishment of normality: On 'lingua franca' English and conversation analysis. *Journal of Pragmatics*, *26*(2), 237–259.

Gallagher, S., & Zahavi, D. (2012). *The phenomenological mind*. Routledge. doi:10.4324/9780203086599

Goodwin, C. (2007). Participation, stance and affect in the organization of activities. *Discourse & Society*, *18*(1), 53–73.

Goodwin, C., & Goodwin, M. H. (2004). Participation. In A. Duranti (Ed.), *A companion to linguistic anthropology* (pp. 222–244). Blackwell-Wiley.

Goodwin, M. H. (1995). Co-construction in girls' hopscotch. *Research on Language and Social Interaction*, *28*(3), 261–281.

Goffman, E. (1981). The lecture. In E. Goffman (Ed.), *Forms of talk* (pp. 162–195). University of Pennsylvania Press.

Hazel, S. (2014). Cultivating objects in interaction: Visual motifs as meaning making practices. In M. Nevile, P. Haddingston, T. Heinemann, & M. Rauniomaa (Eds.), *Interacting with objects: Language, materiality and social activity* (pp. 169–194). John Benjamins.

Heritage, J. (2012). Epistemics in action: Action formation and territories of knowledge. *Research on Language & Social Interaction*, *45*(1), 1–29. doi:10.1080/08351813.2012.646684

Heritage, J., & Maynard, D. W. (2006). Introduction: Analyzing interaction between doctors and patients in primary care encounters. In J. Heritage & D. W. Maynard (Eds.), *Communication in medical care: Interaction between primary care physicians and patients. Studies in interactive sociolinguistics* (Vol. 20, pp. 1–21). Cambridge University Press.

Hofstede, G. (1986). Cultural differences in teaching and learning. *International Journal of Intercultural Relations*, *10*(3), 301–320. doi:10.1016/0147-1767(86)90015-5

Housley, W., & Fitzgerald, R. (2015). Introduction to membership categorisation analysis. In R. Fitzgerald & W. Housley (Eds.), *Advances in membership categorisation analysis* (pp. 1–21). Sage.

Jefferson, G. (1984). Transcription notation. In J. Atkinson & J. Heritage (Eds.), *Structures of social interaction* (pp. 346–369). Cambridge University Press.

Jenkins, J. (2011). Accommodating (to) ELF in the international university. *Journal of Pragmatics*, *43*(4), 926–936. doi:10.1016/j.pragma.2010.05.011

Kidwell, M. (2013). Framing, grounding, and coordinating conversational interaction: Posture, gaze, facial expression, and movement in space. Body – Language – Communication. In A. Cienki, E. Fricke, D. McNeill, & C. Müller (Eds.), *An international handbook on multimodality in human interaction* (pp. 100–112). Mouton de Gruyter.

Klemenčič, M. (2017). From student engagement to student agency: Conceptual considerations of European policies on student-centred learning in higher education. *Higher Education Policy*, *30*(1), 69–85.

Latour, B. (2005). *Reassembling the social: An introduction to actor-network-theory*. Oxford University Press.

Levinson, S. C. (1992). Activity types and language. In P. Drew & J. Heritage (Eds.), *Talk at work: Interaction in institutional settings* (pp. 66–100). Cambridge University Press.

Lim, F. V., O'Halloran, K. L., & Podlasov, A. (2012). Spatial pedagogy: Mapping meanings in the use of classroom space. *Cambridge Journal of Education*, *42*(2), 235–251. doi:10.1080/0305764X.2012.676629

Macaro, E. (2018). *English medium instruction* (1st ed.). Oxford University Press.

Malavska, V. (2016). Genre of an academic lecture. *International Journal on Language, Literature and Culture in Education*, *3*(2), 56–84.

Matsumoto, Y., & Canagarajah, S. (2020). The use of gesture, gesture hold, and gaze in trouble-in-talk among multilingual interlocutors in an. *Journal of Pragmatics*, *169*, 245–267. https://orcid.org/0000-0002-6440-6400

Mondada, L. (2016). Challenges of multimodality: Language and the body in social interaction. *Journal of Sociolinguistics*, *20*(3), 336–366.

Mori, J. (2004). Negotiating sequential boundaries and learning opportunities: A case from a Japanese language classroom. *The Modern Language Journal*, *88*(4), 536–550.

Norris, S. (2004). *Analyzing multimodal interaction: A methodological framework*. Routledge.

Pekarek Doehler, S. (2002). Mediation revisited: The interactive organization of mediation in learning environments. *Mind, Culture, and Activity*, *9*(1), 22–42. doi:10.1207/S15327884MCA0901_03

Sacks, H. (1984). On doing "being ordinary". In J. Atkinson (Ed.), *Structures of social action: Studies in emotion and social interaction* (pp. 413–429). Cambridge University Press. doi:10.1017/CBO9780511665868.024

Sacks, H. (1992). The MIR membership categorization device. In G. Jefferson (Ed.), *Lectures on conversation volumes I and II* (pp. 40–49). Blackwell Publishing.

Sacks, H., Schegloff, E. A., & Jefferson, G. (1974). A simplest systematics for the organization of turn-taking for conversation. *Language*, *50*(4), 696–735.

Schegloff, E. A. (2007). *Sequence organization in interaction*. Cambridge University Press.

Seedhouse, P. (2004). The organisation of language classroom interaction: Conversation analysis methodology. *Language Learning*, *54*(51), 181–222.

Stivers, T., Mondada, L., & Steensig, J. (2011). Knowledge, morality and affiliation in social interaction. In T. Stivers, L. Mondada, & J. Steensig (Eds.), *The morality of knowledge in conversation* (pp. 3–24). Cambridge University Press.

Straus, E. W. (1952). The upright posture. *Psychiatry Quarterly*, *26*(4), 529–556. ISSN. 0033–2720.

Yin, R. K. (2009). *Case study research: Design and methods* (Vol. 5). Sage.

Appendix 1

Standard CA Symbols for Features of Speech (Jefferson, 1984)

Symbol	Name	Use
[text]	Square brackets	marks start and end, respectively, overlapping talk
=	Equal sign	Indiscernible break between utterance lines
(# of seconds)	Timed pause	The hashtag indicates the number of seconds or fraction of a second
(.)	Micro pause	Brief speech "beat" pause
↓	Down arrow	Falling pitch or intonation
↑	Up arrow	Rising pitch or intonation
°text°	Degree symbol	Indicates reduced volume, quiet speech or whisper
text	Underlined text	Indicates the speaker is emphasising or stressing the speech
::::	Colon(s)	Prolongation of a sound
/text/	Forward slashes	Non-standard pronunciation

7 EMI Materials Development
Scaffolding Learning of Linguistics in a BA Programme

Darío Luis Banegas

Introduction

In the broad territory of academia, English is the language often selected to disseminate knowledge and push the frontiers of understanding. Despite valid reservations around linguicism, racism and the hegemonic discourses which may be embedded in knowledge flow and democracy amplified and/or constrained through the use of English (Flores, 2020; Mahboob & Szenes, 2010; Phillipson, 2009), universities around the world have started to offer English-medium courses for both international and national students (Airey et al., 2017). As a consequence of this relatively new phenomenon, English-Medium Instruction (EMI) has emerged as a strategic move in higher education to open new markets and provide students with opportunities at transnational level (Rose & McKinley, 2018). Despite this promising panorama, scholars have noted that EMI seems to fail to provide clear linguistic aims to make EMI sustainable, successful and inclusive (Lasagabaster & Doiz, 2021).

While EMI has "no definitional attention to language learning" (Rose, 2021, p. 145), EMI scholars (e.g. Lasagabaster & Doiz, 2021; Rose, 2021) recognise that lack of English language proficiency may have a negative impact on EMI experiences. Even when there are other approaches that attend to content and language such as content and language integrated learning (CLIL) or integrating content and language in higher education (ICLHE) (Dafouz & Smit, 2020), EMI still needs the deployment of informed practices that support learning through scaffolding strategies that develop students' disciplinary literacies (Malmström & Pecorari, 2021), that is, academic English, for deeper learning (Coyle & Meyer, 2021). Against this backdrop, the aim of this chapter is to understand the criteria I adopted as a tutor/lecturer to design and deliver teaching resources for an undergraduate module on linguistics at a UK university.

DOI: 10.4324/9781003258407-7

Conceptual Background

With the acceleration of EMI in higher education (e.g. Galloway, 2020) and the need to provide students with language support within EMI (Rose, 2021), practice shows a plethora of instructional types in EMI (Schmidt-Unterberger, 2018). Despite heterogeneous delivery, it is agreed that scaffolding learning is vital to ensure the effectiveness of EMI. In this study, the metaphorical term "scaffolding" is approached from a sociocultural theory perspective (Vygotsky, 1962). Scaffolding can be minimally defined as "temporary adaptive support" (Shvarts & Bakker, 2019, p. 5) which can take the form of tutor or peer guidance in interaction or through other mediating tools such as materials that enable students to engage in independent learning and assume greater responsibility with learning tasks in the future. In this regard, scaffolding is a form of planned intervention that can be provided to students (Lantolf & Poehner, 2014) and is associated with the emergence of the zone of proximal development (ZPD), that is, collaboratively mediated interaction. During ZPD, learning leads to individual development as students achieve more than they could have accomplished if they had worked alone. In the context of this study, I mobilise scaffolding to the support provided in and through my teaching resources.

In EMI, materials play a pivotal role in assisting learning. While EMI entails the deployment of authentic (not pedagogically modified) materials *ab initio*, challenges around EMI implementation due to lack of bespoke materials have been recognised in the literature (e.g. Galloway, 2020). Different scholars have also identified the necessity of providing students with support in relation to discipline-specific language, academic discourse, research writing and strategies for effective communication during, for example, presentations (Airey et al., 2017; Farrell, 2020; Schmidt-Unterberger, 2018). In a literature review of EMI, Galloway (2020) suggests that temporary support to EMI students can include using visual aids or explaining complex terms with common words among other techniques.

A few studies have recently discussed EMI materials development. Chou (2017) examined the use of authentic materials in a law school in Taiwan to enhance oral presentations of real cases and subsequent case-based interaction. Kao and Liao (2017) investigated two EMI courses in the humanities to understand how tutors grappled with creating their own materials. Drawing on interviews, teaching notes and course syllabi analysis, the tutors reportedly employed strategies such as visualisation and glocalisation to respond to their context as well as students' needs. In an action research-based project, Cao and Yuan (2020) delineated the EMI principles and practices underpinning a marketing course at a Chinese university. The authors found that the tutors created materials relevant to China and instrumented general academic as well as disciplinary language scaffolds throughout the course. More recently, Banegas and Manzur Busleimán (2021) drew on data collected at an online teacher education programme in Argentina to determine three scaffolding strategies: (1) text simplification (e.g. use of shorter sentences) and rediscursification (e.g. producing a bullet-point list from an argumentative text), (2) use of multimodal resources and (3) sequencing of sources of input and tasks from less to more cognitively and linguistically demanding. On the basis of these strategies and other features identified in course delivery, the authors put forward three principles for EMI materials:

1) Tutor engagement and agency: This refers to the tutor's ability to plan and carry out informed decisions that consider context, personalisation, students' prior knowledge and the provision of opportunities for language development.
2) Purposeful multimodality: This principle pertains to the use of tasks based on multimodal resources and texts that enable students to access input and engage in output. Such multimodal tasks make disciplinary literacies salient.
3) Autonomous learning: Through this principle, students are supported in self-managing content as well as language development through self-access and self-paced resources together with activities that promote reflection and self-assessment.

While the scaffolding strategies and principles described earlier and those explored in the remainder of the chapter may not be intrinsic to EMI, they can still be helpful to EMI tutors, particularly those with limited training in pedagogy and teaching methods.

Research Methodology

This investigation adopted a teacher research perspective. Teacher research is an umbrella term that refers to "systematic self-study" (Borg & Sanchez, 2015, p. 1) carried out by teachers in their own context for the improvement of the teaching and learning processes that unfold in a specific educational environment. Teacher research can take many forms, such as (exploratory) action research (e.g. Banegas & Consoli, 2020; Smith & Rebolledo, 2018) or exploratory practice (e.g. Hanks, 2017) among other notions. Farrell (2020) suggests that EMI lecturers can enhance their reflective practice by engaging in action research. In this chapter, I adopt a descriptive-exploratory perspective as I wish to understand my criteria and informed decisions to design and implement materials for delivering an undergraduate module on linguistics. While being an insider places me in a privileged position to make sense of the overall contexts in which teaching and research coalesce, I recognise the potential bias of being the researcher and the researched.

Context and Participants

This study took place between January and April 2021 at a UK university. While this setting may not be seen as a typical EMI environment since the course was offered at a UK university, thus being English the default language of instruction, in this case, both the students and myself as their lecturer engaged in academic discourse through a language, English, which was not our L1.

I led a module called Introduction to Linguistics at a bespoke four-year EMI humanities course for a group of Omani students. The module spanned over eight weeks and it included the following topics: origins and features of human languages, approaches to linguistics, phonetics and phonology, syntax and morphology, grammar awareness and language noticing, semantics and pragmatics, discourse analysis, sociolinguistics, and intercultural communicative competence. The students submitted their final assignment, an essay in which they had to analyse a teaching resource of their choice under the light of linguistics concepts, in April 2021. Due to COVID-19 restrictions, module delivery was carried out through a virtual learning environment (VLE) for asynchronous input (pre-recorded lectures) and activities (e.g. forums and multiple choice exercises) as well as online synchronous seminars (including group presentations on a given topic) via Zoom.

The participants were ten Omani students, and it was their first time in the UK. In the group, there were nine men and one woman, and their average age was 21. Their studies were fully funded by the Omani government and, once graduated, they were to take up posts in different sectors in Oman. They had all successfully passed the IELTS exam, which is a mandatory requirement to study at a UK university. While their spoken English was satisfactory, they exhibited problems with academic writing at the levels of sentence construction, textual organisation and use of referencing. Prior to their course in the UK, the students had not attended EMI or English for Academic Purposes courses in Oman. They had recently finished secondary education, and their knowledge of English mainly derived from attending traditional English as a foreign language courses in their secondary education. Thus, the bespoke programme in which the Introduction to Linguistics course was included was their first EMI experience.

Data Collection and Analysis

All the students agreed to participate in the study and signed a consent form, which described their role in the study and outlined ethical procedures such as anonymity, confidentiality and potential coercion. This investigation relied on three sources of data collection:

- Teaching artefacts: These included pre-recorded lectures, presentation slides, activities, course material for input, and written formative feedback on students' coursework.
- Tutor journal: I kept a journal during design and delivery of the module. My entries concentrated on my decisions for materials development and reactions to the students' navigation of the module. In total, I wrote 32 entries, with a mean length of 438 words.
- Group discussions: I held three Zoom breakout-room discussions with the students in Weeks 4 and 8 at the end of the seminar. These were about 15 minutes long and we discussed questions such as the following: What materials did you find more helpful/challenging to understand and express the new knowledge in English?

Data were scrutinised by means of thematic analysis (Clarke & Braun, 2016). Thematic analysis was conceived as an iterative process of reading and re-reading the data for initial and axial coding (Saldaña, 2021). The codes led to the setting of a codebook which was used to re-analyse the data. With the aim of ensuring confirmability, trustworthiness and transparency (Lincoln & Guba, 1985), an external researcher acted as a second rater of 60% of the data collected. We discussed discrepancies and reached an interrater agreement of 82%, a figure we considered acceptable.

Findings and Discussion

In this section, findings are organised according to the categories identified in the thematic analysis of the three data collection instruments.

Scaffolding Through Module Organisation

The module combined authentic sources of input such as Rowe and Levine (2018) and Yule (2020), and my own teaching-made resources:

- Pre-recorded lectures: Each one-hour lecture was broken down into two shorter videos with captions. Each video was accompanied with the lecture slides and references.

- Activities: Activities were designed around the lectures and seminars. While some of them could be completed synchronously individually or in groups, others could be completed asynchronously and individually.

As a result of the COVID-19 pandemic, the module was delivered entirely online. I utilised the university virtual learning environment to organise the content of each week in a manner that supported students' navigation and engagement with the new knowledge before and after the Zoom-supported live seminar. For example, in Week 2 of the module, the topic was understanding linguistics as a science (Figure 7.1).

In my journal, I expressed my doubts about the module organisation on the VLE as to me it still looked like a linear repository of documents and activities. However, the students had a different view:

> It really helps to have every week organised according to what happens when. It gives me a clear sense of structure, and the numbered items help me locate things more easily. I also know that the "extend" section

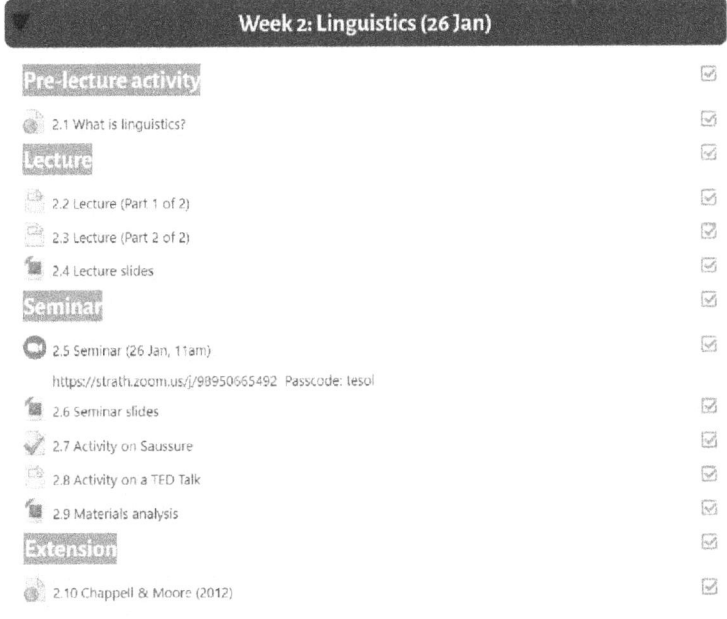

Figure 7.1 Screenshot of session organisation

is optional, so I can do it after the seminar or perhaps another day, or not do it at all.

(Marya, Extract 1)

I tried to imitate the module organisation in my own studying. It's very different from I'm used to, and everything is in English, so it serves two purposes: organisation and language learning.

(Rohan, Extract 2)

The module organisation appeared to have had a positive influence on the students' academic development as they honed their study skills while acquiring academic literacy, an issue frequently identified as a challenge in the EMI literature (e.g. Galloway, 2020).

Scaffolding Through Attention to Disciplinary Literacy

I provided students with supporting opportunities to familiarise themselves with disciplinary terminology. For example, before the lecture, students were asked to find the meaning and pronunciation of these keywords: audio-lingual, determinism, neuroplasticity, relativity and systemic. They also had to label them according to word class and provide a translation into Arabic.

The lecture slides exhibited extensive use of graphic organisers (Figure 7.2) and bullet points (Figure 7.3) to direct students' attention to key concepts in terms of both disciplinary knowledge and subject-specific vocabulary.

In a similar vein, activities provided students with opportunities for focusing on language learning by completing definitions (Figure 7.4) or selecting options to finish off sentences as a way to summarise the main concepts covered in a video (Figure 7.5).

The students exhibited a positive attitude to activities of this nature since they recognised a balance between cognitive demand and linguistic load in its productive phase and a sequential progression of activities. In the group discussion, a student said,

> Because some of the activities at the beginning of the module were more guided and like listening activities [e.g., Figure 7.5], I could concentrate more on the video, the main concepts, and key vocabulary. That made me less anxious as I wasn't expected to write a summary. That happened later once we become comfortable with the new knowledge and all the key linguistic terms.
>
> (Abdul, Extract 3)

EMI Materials Development 89

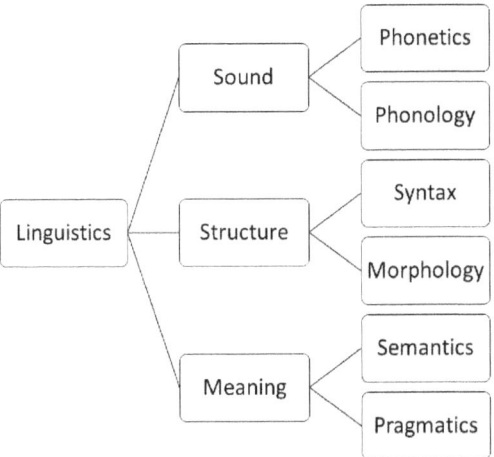

Figure 7.2 Use of graphic organisers

Figure 7.3 Use of bullet points

Similarly, another student added,

> I think that having the key terms foregrounded allowed me to pay more attention to specific vocabulary I need to use in writing and speaking when talking about linguistics. The use of graphic organisers and list of key words have been really helpful to me.
>
> (Omar, Extract 4)

1.2 Definitions of language

Drag the words into the correct boxes

Language is _____ upon words _____ into _____.
Language can also be defined as _____ property, and therefore _____.
Last, we can also say that language is _____ of signs.

- an exclusive human
- sentences
- and the combination of words
- a system
- a human artefact
- a system of communication based

○ Check

Figure 7.4 Completion activity

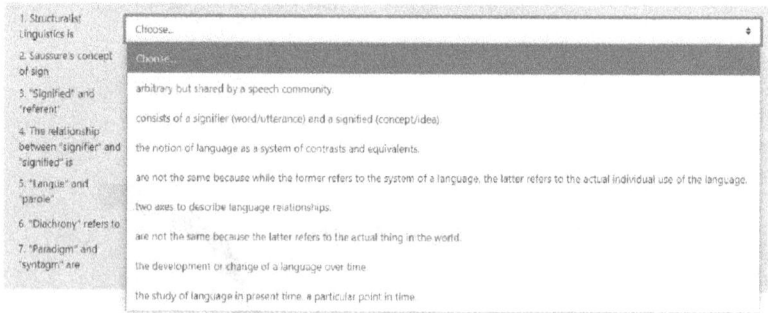

1. Structuralist Linguistics is	Choose...
2. Saussure's concept of sign	Choose...
3. "Signified" and "referent"	arbitrary but shared by a speech community.
4. The relationship between "signifier" and "signified" is	consists of a signifier (word/utterance) and a signified (concept/idea).
5. "Langue" and "parole"	the notion of language as a system of contrasts and equivalents.
6. "Diachrony" refers to	are not the same because while the former refers to the system of a language, the latter refers to the actual individual use of the language.
7. "Paradigm" and "syntagm" are	two axes to describe language relationships.
	are not the same because the latter refers to the actual thing in the world.
	the development or change of a language over time.
	the study of language in present time, a particular point in time.

Figure 7.5 Video-based activity

The design of tailored-made activities to draw students' attention to general as well as specific vocabulary succeeded at responding to their linguistic needs (Kao & Liao, 2017). Such activities became language scaffolds, as Cao and Yuan (2020) recommend, which also provided learners with support to incorporate disciplinary terminology, an issue often reported in the literature (e.g. Farrell, 2020; Schmidt-Unterberger, 2018). The students' self-reported acquisition of new terms was a feature I noted in my journal after they delivered group presentations in which they had to discuss a journal article:

> Most of them have come a long way! From our first interactions in class to today, I've noted how they make every effort to use general academic language and make appropriate use of terminology. In her presentation today, Marya did not use the word "sounds" but "phonemes"

or "allophones" to describe specific linguistic features of spoken language.

(Author, Extract 5)

While providing support with disciplinary vocabulary was important, I was aware of my interest and the students' need to move beyond sentential level and engage with genre awareness and writing at textual level. I had been made aware that they struggled with completing longer pieces of work for previous modules and that some of them had failed because of being unable to submit their assignment or because their Turnitin score yielded a high percentage of plagiarism (above 20%). Thus, in order to support students with writing conventions and succeeding at essay writing as expected in a UK university, I provided them with a set of guidelines (Figure 7.6) to write their final assignment.

The main aim of the assignment briefing was to provide them with a structure they could employ to organise their writing. In one seminar, I also provided them with a list of the best journals in linguistics and language according to Scimago and asked them to complete short activities so that they navigated these journals. I also reminded them of the library support the university offers and directed them to YouTube videos on using APA 7th edition. Despite my efforts to make them independent, the students asked me for sample essays from previous years. Since the module was new, I could not offer any past assignments. However, in the last seminar, I devoted one hour to offering advice on structure and phrases they could use to introduce concepts, establish relationships and present their own reflections. In my journal, I noted,

> Maybe I should have included more language awareness raising activities alongside articles to orient their attention to language they could use to fulfil different functions. Or I could have written a sample essay myself, but then everyone would feel that they need to follow that sample, as if it were the only option, and that could influence the topic they choose to discuss in their analysis.

(Author, Extract 6)

On this issue, one of the students expressed,

> Having a skeleton to follow is really useful, even the questions or the order in which we need to write is handy. And suggested length of each section is great because it gives me a sense of where I should do better. But it is still difficult for me to imagine the actual essay. The content, the analysis, and the level of language I need to use. This is why a sample essay would be helpful.

(Samir, Extract 7)

> By means of a 1,500-word essay, you will critique one existing language teaching resource (e.g., a series of tasks, a worksheet, a coursebook page, an app and an online activity) designed to help English language learners to develop competence in one dimension (e.g., lexis, pronunciation, grammar and listening skills) of language teaching. You will critically assess one such resource from the perspective of the knowledge about language acquired in the class and the context in which it might be used. Make sure that every section in your essay includes a numbered heading. That contributes to organisation and clarity.
>
> Suggested structure of the essay:
> Title: (e.g., "A critique of a teaching resource")
> Introduction (30–50 words): State the aim of the essay (What specific focus/branch of Linguistics will you use to analyse the resource?)
> A brief description of the resource (include the resource itself or a link if appropriate, acknowledge full reference to it) and the context in which it appears to be used if known (150–200 words).
> Analysis of the resource in one specific dimension (1,200 words): first, briefly state how your analysis is organised, that is, what specific aspects you will analyse; secondly, analyse each aspect providing theoretical support and including specific examples from the resource. Tip: each paragraph should focus on one aspect at a time.
> Conclusion (50 words): Return to the aim of the essay and reflect on the extent you have achieved it and how.
> References (APA 7th ed.): Please use high-quality references. High-quality references typically refer to published works which are seminal or within the last 5–10 years. They can be peer-reviewed journal articles, peer-reviewed book chapters, monographs, edited books, government reports and so on. A good starting point are the references your tutors have used in their slides, the class reading list and further suggested reading.

Figure 7.6 Assignment briefing

Extract 7 shows that despite the efforts made to scaffold disciplinary discourse, academic writing continued to be an area which had to be further tailored to meet the students' needs.

Scaffolding Through Localisation

Scaffolding was also employed by including forums in every other unit through which students could discuss linguistics topics in relation to their context or individual learning trajectories. Here, I list some of the questions discussed in the module forums:

- In this forum, share a link to a video which explains what language is. Tell us why you have found it particularly helpful in terms of content and language.
- Which variety of English seems to be preferred in Oman? Why? How do you feel about this? How does it reflect what we discussed today (sociolinguistics)?

In the group discussions, the students agreed that making the activities connected to their personal ways of learning or linking them to their context (Oman), and learning disciplinary knowledge and language became important. One student said,

> I think that by asking us to analyse sources from Oman made learning linguistics relevant. I paid more attention to the content and the specialised knowledge because I wanted to be accurate. Learning became meaningful and easier because I felt motivated to work on the analysis.
>
> (Amal, Extract 8)

Amal's words capture the benefit of localising EMI courses as already reported in the literature (e.g. Cao & Yuan, 2020; Kao & Liao, 2017). Without being a specific EMI strategy, localisation had a positive impact on student motivation and engagement as the students found the new knowledge and overall learning experience meaningful.

In sum, the analysis presented earlier shows that there was a tendency to scaffold (1) content of linguistics and (2) academic as well as disciplinary discourse through learner-centred, multimodal resources and activities. In this regard, scaffolding central aspects such as genre awareness (essay), subject-specific terminology or transferable skills development by enabling students to carry out activities that localised the new knowledge (conceptual and procedural) was possible given my deployment of tutor engagement and agency, purposeful modality and instances of autonomous learning (Banegas & Manzur Busleimán, 2021), which became instrumental in online education. In addition, localisation exerted a positive influence as a scaffolding strategy for content learning.

It should be stressed that purposeful modality became prominent and influential as it allowed students to navigate different genres with increasing degrees of complexity while attending to disciplinary literacy at the same time. In addition, autonomous learning acquired a special place in the architecture of the module as students could (1) watch the pre-recorded lectures at their own pace, take notes on content and language, watch them with subtitles and return to them if necessary, (2) complete the forums and other individual activities at their own pace. This gave them the opportunity to edit their work for clarity and accuracy.

Conclusion

This small-scale study shows that in EMI courses, materials (sources of input, activities and assignments) need to be tailored to support students' disciplinary knowledge and literacy. Content learning and disciplinary language are inseparable, and issues with the latter may have a negative effect on the former. Thus, this chapter is an invitation for EMI tutors to engage in materials development that attends to both content and English language learning through the use of different scaffolding strategies. These scaffolding strategies may refer to content organisation, disciplinary literacy and topic localisation. Many of these strategies could be transferred from instruction in the dominant language or approaches such as CLIL or ICLHE to enhance the mechanics of deeper learning (Coyle & Meyer, 2021) in EMI environments. Notwithstanding, it should be acknowledged that the positive effects of the scaffolding strategies discussed earlier are only based on self-reporting.

Future lines of inquiry can engage in triangulating participants' self-reported effects on academic writing with syntactic complexity and textual analysis of their written assignments. In addition, future studies can further explore teacher research as a means to understand the dynamics of materials development, adaptation and use according to varying circumstances. In the same line, future research can particularly examine online, blended or hybrid modes of learning and study how students use asynchronous resources and engage in the collaborative construction of knowledge. For example, it would be beneficial to understand the extent to which students participate in online forums by means of social network analysis.

References

Airey, J., Lauridsen, K. M., Räsänen, A., Salö, L., & Schwach, V. (2017). The expansion of English-medium instruction in the Nordic countries: Can top-down university language policies encourage bottom-up disciplinary literacy goals? *Higher Education, 73*(4), 561–576. https://doi.org/10.1007/s10734-015-9950-2

Banegas, D. L., & Consoli, S. (2020). Action research in language education. In J. McKinley & H. Rose (Eds.), *The Routledge handbook of research methods in applied linguistics* (pp. 176–187). Routledge.

Banegas, D. L., & Manzur Busleimán, G. (2021). EMI materials in online initial English language teacher education. In D. Lasagabaster & A. Doiz (Eds.),

Language use in English-medium instruction at university: International perspectives on teacher practice (pp. 100–125). Routledge.

Borg, S., & Sanchez, H. S. (Eds.). (2015). International perspectives on teacher research. Palgrave.

Cao, H., & Yuan, R. (2020). Promoting English as a medium of instruction in university teaching: An action research experience. Journal of Education for Teaching, 46(2), 240–243. https://doi.org/10.1080/02607476.2020.1724657

Chou, J. T. (2017). Use of authentic materials in law school. In W. Tsou & S.-M. Kao (Eds.), English as a medium of instruction in higher education (pp. 131–145). Springer.

Clarke, V., & Braun, V. (2016). Thematic analysis. In E. Lyons & A. Coyle (Eds.), Analysing qualitative data in psychology (2nd ed, pp. 84–103). Sage.

Coyle, D., & Meyer, O. (2021). Beyond CLIL: Pluriliteracies teaching for deeper learning. Cambridge University Press.

Dafouz, E., & Smit, U. (Eds.). (2020). ROAD-MAPPING English medium education in the internationalised university. Palgrave.

Farrell, T. S. C. (2020). Professional development through reflective practice for English-medium instruction (EMI) teachers. International Journal of Bilingual Education and Bilingualism, 23(3), 277–286. https://doig.org/10.1080/13670050.2019.1612840

Flores, N. (2020). From academic language to language architecture: Challenging raciolinguistic ideologies in research and practice. Theory into Practice, 59(1), 22–31. https://doi.org/10.1080/00405841.2019.1665411

Galloway, N. (Ed.). (2020). English in higher education – English medium part 1: Literature review. The British Council.

Hanks, J. (2017). Exploratory practice in language teaching: Puzzling about principles and practices. Palgrave.

Kao, S.-M., & Liao, H.-T. (2017). Developing glocalised materials for EMI courses in humanities. In W. Tsou & S.-M. Kao (Eds.), English as a medium of instruction in higher education (pp. 147–162). Springer.

Lantolf, J. P., & Poehner, M. E. (2014). Sociocultural theory and the pedagogical imperative in L2 education: Vygotskian praxis and the research/practice divide. Routledge.

Lasagabaster, D., & Doiz, A. (Eds.). (2021). Language use in English-medium instruction at university: International perspectives on teacher practice. Routledge.

Lincoln, Y., & Guba, E. (1985). Naturalistic inquiry. Sage.

Mahboob, A., & Szenes, E. (2010). Linguicism and racism in assessment practices in higher education. Linguistics and Human Sciences, 3(3), 325–354. https://doi.org/10.1558/lhs.v3i3.325

Malmström, H., & Pecorari, D. (2021). Epilogue: Disciplinary literacies as a nexus for content and language teacher practice. In D. Lasagabaster & A. Doiz (Eds.), Language use in English-medium instruction at university: International perspectives on teacher practice (pp. 213–221). Routledge.

Phillipson, R. (2009). English in globalisation, a lingua franca or a lingua frankensteinia? TESOL Quarterly, 43(2), 335–339. https://doi.org/10.1002/j.1545-7249.2009.tb00175.x

Rose, H. (2021). Students' language-related challenges of studying through English: What EMI teachers can do. In D. Lasagabaster & A. Doiz (Eds.), Language use in

English-medium instruction at university: International perspectives on teacher practice (pp. 145–166). Routledge.

Rose, H., & McKinley, J. (2018). Japan's English-medium instruction initiatives and the globalization of higher education. *Higher Education, 75*(1), 111–129. https://doi.org/10.1007/s10734-017-0125-1

Rowe, B., & Levine, D. (2018). *A concise introduction to linguistics* (5th ed.). Routledge.

Saldaña, J. (2021). *The coding manual for qualitative researchers* (4th ed.). Sage.

Schmidt-Unterberger, B. (2018). The English-medium paradigm: A conceptualisation of English-medium teaching in higher education. *International Journal of Bilingual Education and Bilingualism, 21*(5), 527–539. https://doi.org/10.1080/13670050.2018.1491949

Smith, R., & Rebolledo, P. (2018). *A handbook for exploratory action research*. The British Council.

Shvarts, A., & Bakker, A. (2019). The early history of the scaffolding metaphor: Bernstein, Luria, Vygotsky, and before. *Mind, Culture, and Activity, 26*(1), 4–23. https://doig.org/10.1080/10749039.2019.1574306

Vygotsky, L. S. (1962). *Thought and language*. MIT Press.

Yule, G. (2020). *The study of language* (7th ed.). Cambridge University Press.

8 Online Input and EMI Pedagogy in the COVID-19 Pandemic in Italy

Francesca Costa and Olivia Mair

Introduction

The COVID-19 pandemic (ongoing at the time of writing) has had an unexpected impact on all areas of life, including, of course, education. In February 2020, Italy was the first country in Europe to face this emergency following the identification of major outbreaks of COVID-19. Universities and schools began to close around 24 February 2020. There was an immediate reaction to the emergency, and synchronous and asynchronous online or ERT (Emergency Remote Teaching) courses were activated within a week in some universities. In time for the start of the 2020–2021 academic year, universities equipped themselves to provide courses that were either hybrid (both in-class and online) or exclusively online, but which for the most part were synchronous. Many types of platforms were used for these courses including Blackboard Collaborate, Google Meet, Teams, Webex and Zoom among others.

EMI (English-Medium Instruction) courses, which were already growing in terms of the number of courses and the research dedicated to them before the pandemic (Block & Khan, 2021; Bowles & Murphy, 2020; Carrió-Pastor & Bellés-Fortuño, 2021; Dimova & Kling, 2020; Lasagabaster & Doiz, 2021; Paulsrud et al., 2021; Rubio-Alcalá & Coyle, 2021), also faced the switch to online teaching. Even before the arrival of COVID-19, some scholars had suggested the need to focus on online EMI settings, and not only on face-to-face lectures (Querol-Julián & Crawford Camiciottoli, 2019).

It has become clear that the pandemic has provided an opportunity to investigate new forms and contexts for EMI. This study, therefore, identifies and explores the features of online EMI input during the pandemic. The research gap in this area is self-evident, even if there were projects already in place before the pandemic on language and content-based e-learning techniques (https://incollabeu.wixsite.com/project/outputs). To date, only

DOI: 10.4324/9781003258407-8

one other study (Cicillini & Giacosa, 2020a, 2020b) has dealt with the topic of EMI teaching and learning during the pandemic in Italy. However, research has been carried out on input in online EFL (English as a Foreign Language) contexts in Italy, addressing similar issues (Borro & Scolaro, 2021; Giacosa, 2021; Conti, 2021).

For these reasons, data collection was carried out during the pandemic by means of a questionnaire sent to EMI lecturers, followed by two stimulated recall sessions linked to two video lectures. At the methodological level, stimulated recall has rarely been used (Tai, 2021) for EMI research. The aim of the study is to investigate the experience of online teaching by EMI lecturers during the pandemic in Italy and to analyse the type of input used in order to understand how the EMI online format differs from face-to-face EMI settings. Following the introduction, the chapter reviews the available literature regarding EMI online, describes the methodology and presents the results of the questionnaire and video-stimulated recall interviews.

Online EMI Input

This section reviews the literature on EMI input and online EMI teaching, with some reference to online teaching in non-EMI contexts. It takes into account multimodal, linguistic and pedagogical input.

In EMI teaching contexts, a range of instructional strategies may be adopted to enhance comprehensibility, improve second language acquisition and facilitate content learning. Lecturer input may include speech modification (through pace changes, dynamic variation and emphasis), lexical input in the form of keywords, glossaries, synonyms, definitions and paraphrasing, changes to the way information is presented and structured, or extra-linguistic aspects including the use of ICT and incorporation of active learning practices (Coonan, 2012; Costa, 2016; Costa & Mariotti, 2021). Using video-stimulated recall to investigate the strategies used in the EMI classroom and the extent to which they aligned with institutional language policy, Quick (2021, p. 65) found that each participant used "a variety of pedagogical strategies to enhance learning in the EMI classroom, including the use of anecdotes, demonstrations, exercises, experiments and quizzes". Some aspects of lecturer input, such as comprehension checks and questions open up opportunities for negotiation of meaning and potentially enhance student engagement (Morell, 2020). A view of language as comprising not just written and spoken language but also visual elements, typographical features, gestural cues, facial expression, eye contact and posture means that multimodal aspects of communication are recognised forms of input (Morell, 2018).

Research has shown that in EMI contexts, lecturers may need to make language adjustments and adopt effective use of multisemiotic resources in order to meet students' needs and improve comprehensibility (Crawford Camiciottoli & Fortanet-Gómez, 2015; Fortanet-Gómez & Ruiz-Madrid, 2014; Morell, 2018, 2020; Ruiz Madrid & Valeiras-Jurado, 2020). In an online teaching context, multimodal aspects may become even more critical as teachers also face the constraints of teaching through learning platforms in a video environment. Querol-Julián and Crawford Camiciottoli (2019) assert that in synchronous videoconferencing lectures (SVL), gestural input may become more important because eye contact is not possible. Some gestures may fulfil pragmatic functions, such as stance-taking or intensification (Querol-Julián, 2021). Such non-verbal communication modes are possible within the constraints of SVL, while other types of movement are not.

Student engagement during online teaching was already of growing interest in research on EMI and became a more urgent issue as a result of the pandemic (Cicillini & Giacosa, 2020a, 2020b; Querol-Julián, 2021). An Italian study based on the initial period of the pandemic showed that teachers found students were harder to engage as a result of perceived mental health issues, while students found that the English language proficiency of both lecturers and students affected interaction (Cicillini & Giacosa, 2020a). It should be noted that the study was based on the first months of the pandemic, an unplanned situation in which lecturers, in many cases, had not yet developed appropriate technical competence. Likewise, a study of students' perceptions of learning in EMI study programmes in Turkish universities at the start of the pandemic found that students' psychological distress and level of self-efficacy in English led to overall low satisfaction with remote learning (Yüksel, 2022). Results of the study pointed to the need for "personal and extended interaction opportunities for students" (Yüksel, 2022, p. 359).

Indeed, in the available literature on EMI online, interaction, both of the student–student and student–teacher variety, emerges as the biggest challenge. Some of the difficulties in creating successful online EMI interaction relate to the computer-mediated nature of the communication, while others relate to English language level (Borro & Scolaro, 2021; Yüksel, 2022) or even to culture (Hopkyns, 2021). Borro and Scolaro (2021) highlight the risks of not being able to judge linguistic appropriateness in online contexts due to being unable to see students' facial expressions or gauge their reactions. Teachers have in fact described the sensation of *teaching to a void* (Hopkyns, 2021).

A range of possible lecturer input strategies for coping with the new experience and improving student participation emerge from research. Enhancing comprehensibility through the use of elaborated and modified-elaborated input is one possibility (Borro & Scolaro, 2021). Other options include increased use of repetition and questions, calling for interaction by inviting students to turn on their microphones and camera, and the use of the chat function (Cicillini & Giacosa, 2020a, 2020b). Lecturers also planned more in-class activities and exercises and set up more group work to stimulate interaction among students. As the pandemic evolves, initial concern about students' lack of participation has led lecturers to shift their focus to student engagement (Cicillini & Giacosa, 2020a). A study focused on the Taiwanese context explored "the experiences and challenges" associated with blended EMI courses established in response to the COVID-19 pandemic (Lin et al., 2021, p. 2). Referring to data collected both in the initial period of the pandemic in 2020 and during the following year, the study found that teaching became progressively more student-centred, with greater interaction, group work, technological support for language and flexibility and choice in assessment tasks in response to requests from students. It recommended that in order for EMI online to be successful, careful pedagogical planning and preparation are needed.

In Italy, the circumstances of the COVID-19 pandemic have intensified an already existing need to address the pedagogical aspects of EMI teaching in both face-to-face and online contexts, as Borsetto and Bier (2021) recognise. They argue that in general, teaching approaches in Italy need to become more student-centred, leaving behind the more formal transmission model associated with Italian higher education (Fedeli, 2018). They propose that EMI teaching in both face-to-face and online contexts can be improved through "the conscious adoption of different semiotic modes during face-to-face classes . . . , together with a greater awareness and systematic use of digital media and Information and Communication Technologies (ICT)" (Borsetto & Bier, 2021, p. 109).

Finally, another study by Chiasson et al. (2015, p. 235), while not carried out in an EMI context, found that teachers faced different time management issues when online. Overall, however, the study found that lecturers who taught their courses synchronously, as in the case of this study, "did not see any major differences from teaching the same course in a face-to-face classroom" when it came to interaction and instructional styles. Like the lecturers in Lin et al. (2021), lecturers in Chiasson et al.'s (2015) study tended to develop a less frontal and more student-centred approach over time.

In the final stages of editing, new studies on EMI online were released (Pun et al., 2022). While it is too late to take their arguments fully into account, the fact that they have emerged in a similar time frame to the present work confirms the growing interest in and importance of the digital aspects of EMI and online pedagogy.

Research Questions

This study sought to investigate how lecturers in Italy have responded to online EMI and the adjustments they have made to input and delivery of content. Teachers have indicated in questionnaires that teaching in an EMI context changes pedagogy (Macaro et al., 2020), but how does EMI change when it goes online? Which input strategies do lecturers adopt or modify? Answering these questions may support future online EMI endeavours.

Methodology

This research is mainly qualitative, with some elements of quantitative analysis. The quantitative part, which consisted of an online questionnaire, was carried out before the qualitative one (QUANT→qual), partly because it served to select two lecturers whose video lectures were analysed in a later phase.

Instruments

Two instruments were used for this research: an online questionnaire created using Google Forms and a stimulated recall protocol in which excerpts of the transcriptions, comments and questions from the researchers, and space for the responses of the two lecturers were given.

The questionnaire was in Italian and used closed questions to gather details of the lecturers' teaching experience and online EMI practice such as:

- type of teaching used during the pandemic; comparison of lecture length of online and face-to-face lectures;
- materials;
- assessment;
- opinion of students;
- interaction with students;
- tools used for the first time in the pandemic;
- lecture preparation time;
- course content;
- methodology;
- evaluation of online teaching in comparison to face-to-face teaching;
- use of the native language;
- teaching and learning strategies;
- positive aspects;
- negative aspects;
- satisfaction with online teaching.

Video-stimulated recall (VSR) was chosen as a way to gain deeper, personal insights into lecturer input and practice beyond those afforded by the questionnaire. In stimulated recall interviews, respondents verbalise their thoughts about a task after carrying it out (Dörnyei, 2007). In this study, VSR interviews were carried out by both researchers. As the aim of the research was to investigate EMI practices online, with a specific focus on instructional strategies and input, an interview protocol was prepared in advance, based on key moments in the lectures. Participants watched the video-recording of their own lecture and were asked to comment on their input. The lectures were of the synchronous videoconferencing lecture (SVL) variety, in which instruction occurs in real time and there is interaction between lecturers and students (Martin et al., 2017).

In spite of being time- and labour-intensive, VSR offers deep insight into lecturers' "reflective thinking mechanisms, their beliefs about teaching, and the relationship between beliefs and actions" (Gazdag et al., 2019, pp. 60–61). Quick (2021, p. 65) found that using VSR in EMI professional development was a useful tool to develop lecturers' awareness of "the impact linguistic and pedagogical choices can have on student learning".

Sampling

The study sample is based on the following criteria: criterion sampling (public and private universities in Northern Italy) regarding the questionnaire, and convenience sampling (lecturers who, after completing the questionnaire, were willing to send us their video lectures and participate in the stimulated recall session) regarding the recording of the lectures (Duff, 2008).

The questionnaire was realised with the help of a master's degree student, who prepared the Google Forms version of the questionnaire, which was then sent to EMI lecturers in six Northern Italian universities, two of which were private. The questionnaire was completed by 73 EMI lecturers. Two lecturers from one of the universities agreed to participate in the stimulated recall session and to share a video lecture. Each lecturer gave their informed consent to be recorded and observed for one class session and to be interviewed.

Questionnaire Data Analysis

The age ranges of the lecturers who replied to the questionnaire were 45–54 (32.9%), 35–44 (27.4%), 55–64 (26%), 25–34 (8.2%) and 65–70 (5.5%).

The lecturers belonged to a variety of disciplines across sciences, social sciences, economics and medicine.

Regarding EMI experience before 2020–2021, 47.9% of the participants had taught for two to five years and 42.5% for more than five years. Most of the participants (61.6%) had followed an EMI training course.

The lecturers reported using mainly SVL during the pandemic (64.4%). Some of them (24.7%) said that they used both synchronous and asynchronous lectures, 8.2% gave recorded lectures and 2.7% used slides with audio recordings. For each academic hour, 65.2% of the participants carried out one hour of online lectures, while for 34.8%, it lasted 30–60 minutes. In terms of lesson preparation time when compared to face-to-face lectures, 54.8% of the participants spent more time preparing online lectures and 45.2% of them the same amount. In most cases (56.2%), online learning was adapted to the new requirements, especially regarding the amount of content delivered, while in 41.1% of cases, there were no adaptations. For a minority of lecturers (2.7%), the courses were totally modified. In addition to the lectures, some other material was given to students: in most cases, downloadable slides and, at times, handouts.

Lecturers were asked about their perceptions of student engagement and interaction. While 35.6% of them found students as attentive online as in the classroom, 20.5% said students were attentive at times and 27.4% said they were not able to judge. Only 8.2% found students more attentive, while 8.3% found students very distracted. The majority of lecturers (65.8%) perceived no difference in the amount of interaction between online and face-to-face lectures, while 19.2% thought their online lectures became more interactive and 15% thought their lectures were less interactive. Lecturers interacted with students via questions during the lecture (59%), internal tools of platforms (chat and polls) (26%), tools external to the platform (11%) or in an asynchronous way, for example, with forums (4%).

As for the tools used for the first time during the pandemic (with more than one possible answer), 80.8% used videoconferencing, 64.4% recorded lectures and 30.1% used chats.

Teaching and learning strategies were used differently in online EMI (a question with more than one possible answer). It became evident that questions were the least used strategy during online lessons, followed by group work, while the most used strategies were surveys and quizzes, followed by repetition. Around half of the respondents (56.2%) said they had to repeat things more often to ensure the message had reached the students since there was no feedback in the way there would be in class. Some participants (32.9%) said they had to give clearer instructions about materials and activities and 15.1% said that they had to be more explicit. Only 17.8% said they did not change their strategies.

As for the method considered to be most effective in online distance learning and teaching (more than one possible answer), 61.1% said teaching based on lecturer–student discussion, 28.8% group work and 21.9% involving students in giving presentations.

When asked if using a non-native language to teach online made any difference, 47.9% of the participants said it did not, 21.9% said that they felt less comfortable and 13.7% said that it was more difficult. Only 9.6% said they felt more at ease. The other percentages were very low.

Lecturers were given a list of the opportunities and challenges of EMI online. As far as opportunities were concerned, lecturers cited: students being able to access recorded lectures more than once (54.8%); being able to innovate their teaching (52.1%); the chance to enhance their technical skills (46.6%); the removal of gaps in their schedules and travel expenses (38.4%); not having to deal with behavioural management (19.2%); having more relaxed schedules (15.1%) and the fact that students were more active online (15.1%), and being able to motivate students to seek information on the Internet (11%).

The challenges included the lack of interpersonal relationships with students (cited by 91.8%), a negative development in student behaviour, such as for absences (38.4%), the time needed to learn to use the platforms (13.7%) and a decrease in teaching quality due to the forced use of new technologies (11%). Finally, 4.1% of the participants did not perceive any negative aspects.

The last question regarded the lecturers' satisfaction with online distance learning and teaching: 68.5% said they were satisfied, 23.3% very satisfied, with only 2.7% not satisfied and 5.5% partially satisfied.

Stimulated Recall Analysis

An inductive approach was adopted for analysing the interviews, with coding carried out with the help of Nvivo. First-cycle and second-cycle coding enabled clusters of meaning and themes to emerge. Once complete, both researchers examined the themes and the data to ensure consensus was reached.

Although neither lecturer found major changes in their approach to teaching online through English, they noted a series of subtle changes, which seemed to result in an overall awareness of the constraints of EMI teaching online (T1) and feelings of discomfort (T2). Both felt that they had to make compromises when teaching online:

> The communicative setting is a little bit poorer. I cannot move. I cannot get near them. I cannot put me with them on the same side of the

class, looking at the slides. So something is lost. And so part of it is also consciously trying to compensate for this.

(T1)

I'm sure that the quality of my dual mode classes is lower. . . .. It's a feeling. If I'm not comfortable . . .

(T2)

Overall, teaching online is quite difficult and challenging.

(T2)

Both lecturers perceived a cognitive overload on the part of the online EMI instructor, who needs to deal with student comments via audio and the chat function, as well as with technical problems. Lecturers also needed to deal with the various time zones of international students, in addition to the routine challenges of EMI teaching, such as providing explicit instructions, ensuring content is well-structured and checking comprehension. Teaching online thus adds another layer of complexity to EMI contexts because lecturers feel forced to divide their attention among even more concerns than before.

T1 teaches philosophy and the interview is based on an online lecture that introduces the concept of *laïcité* in France. The extent of T1's reflections, which are at times lengthy and detailed, suggests a deep engagement with both EMI and considerations relating to the diverse backgrounds of the students. Overall, the intentional nature of T1's EMI input and instructional strategy is a strong theme. Input was consciously modified to suit the online context in many areas: keeping more text in slides in case students missed oral input; using the voice to emphasise to a greater extent to compensate for students at times not being able to see his face or gestures; and using slides as a support to ask questions and set up interaction.

As far as linguistic input is concerned, T1 explains that he uses definitions, repetition and discourse markers much like in face-to-face EMI contexts, but in online teaching, he is even more explicit in providing information. He is particularly attentive to reformulation of students' answers in order to overcome any sound problems in computer-mediated communication, and to support the speaker and facilitate comprehension by other students. Codeswitching takes place between French and English as there are French students in the class and the lecturer needs to make it clear that *laïcité* in French and *secularism* in English are not exactly the same. This, he says, would unfold in much the same way as when teaching face to face.

The interview also gives insight into how T1 sets up and supports EMI online interaction. More than once he refers to the way the certainties of the spatial aspects of the physical classroom are disrupted during online, hybrid teaching. The lecturer can no longer move to be among students and when students participate in a discussion, the absence of physical classroom space can affect how they perceive other students:

> During this discussion, they tend to turn and look at the others. And this physically becomes kind of a vivid presentation of the fact that I am expressing this idea from this physical point in the class; you are expressing this idea from another point in class. . . . And so . . . it visualizes this . . . plurality of opinions.
>
> (T1)

When teaching online, input is thus modified to take into account students' difficulties in perceiving reactions and to make sure that they feel "comfortable" and that they are in a "safe space" in which to express themselves. During interactive moments, T1 uses gesture more online, "to reinforce the sense of this safe setting". T2 makes similar reflections about replacing classroom space with virtual teaching and its impact on interaction. He considers that interaction is "more or less the same in small groups but it's more difficult for students who are physically separated and who have never been to the university" (T2).

T2 teaches in the Agricultural Science faculty and the lecture he is asked to comment on is about plant pathogens taught in hybrid mode (with some students in the classroom, but the majority online). By his own account, T2 has a playful and thoughtful approach to pedagogy, in both face-to-face and online contexts. He gives several examples of how he uses humour in the classroom, such as through jokes and word plays: "Humour is something I use to put myself in a comfortable mood to interact", he says. However, he finds it harder to use humour online and in hybrid settings, because he cannot gauge students' reactions through their facial expressions, either due to mask-wearing or cameras being turned off.

Nonetheless, two key moments that he is asked to comment on involve humour. In the first, he presents a slide titled "How to get away with murder" and in the second he sets up a role-play activity in which one student plays a researcher and another, a farmer. He explains that the activity was created entirely for online hybrid teaching to highlight the importance of communication.

> Telephone conversations happen to researchers often as they are constantly asked for advice by farmers. They can create misunderstandings that follow through the whole production chain to food. Students need to use general language to express themselves properly as well

as technical language. I am pushing that a lot. It's one of my learning objectives.

(T2)

During the role-play activity, students laugh and are engaged, so in spite of T1's concerns about using humour, the video-recording shows he managed to overcome the constraints of hybrid teaching to use humour for effective interaction. This suggests a discrepancy between his perception of the difficulty of EMI online and his actual experience.

As regards other linguistic input, T2 checks students' comprehension more frequently in online teaching, because in face-to-face teaching he "could see with [his] eyes if they understood". He asks fewer questions in hybrid mode, favouring the use of polls at the start of class, including exam-type questions. Overall, both lecturers reflect extensively on the altered use of gesture. In some cases, gesture is perceived to have little value and voice variation takes on more importance. During other times, in which the slides are not being shared, or are not taking centre stage on the screen, such as during housekeeping at the start of a lecture, or for discussion with students, gesture may assume greater importance than in face-to-face contexts.

Discussion and Conclusion

Overall, the COVID-19 pandemic and the switch to extended periods of online lecturing have been an impetus for innovation in EMI. The questionnaire showed that over 50% of lecturers considered the chance to innovate their teaching one of the positive aspects. The study reveals a range of changes to lecturer input: increased repetition, more explicit instruction and the increase in use of quizzes and polls on the one hand, with fewer questions and less group work on the other. This finding suggests that EMI professional development for online teaching should focus on group work and interaction, backing up the findings of other studies (Cicillini & Giacosa, 2020b; Lin et al., 2021; Yüksel, 2022). Even so, the majority of respondents believed that they achieved the same level of interaction in online teaching as in face-to-face teaching.

The VSR interviews revealed how changes in gestural input and voice variation lead to a shift in the array of multimodal resources drawn on by lecturers, something they are at times conscious of. Themes emerging from the analysis of interviews with the two lecturers were in line with results from the questionnaire, which showed that lack of interpersonal relationships in online teaching was the most commonly identified negative aspect (by 91.8%), while nearly 70% of respondents considered teaching based on interaction to be the most effective method.

Given that hybrid teaching practices, video lecturing and online EMI teaching are likely to continue well beyond the pandemic, the findings of this paper have implications for the planning and delivery of future EMI courses online. To compensate for a reduction in interpersonal relationships and in quality of interaction, attention needs to be given to enhancing opportunities for student–student interaction through group work. Any EMI training for online or hybrid contexts should focus on designing tasks suitable for group work, supporting comprehensibility through available multi-semiotic resources, and increasing interaction.

Acknowledgements

We would like to thank Marco Concavo for working with us on the questionnaire. This article was developed by both authors. Costa is responsible for Introduction; Instruments; Sampling and Questionnaire data analysis; and Mair for Online EMI input; Research questions; Methodology; Stimulated recall analysis and Conclusion.

References

Block, D., & Khan, S. (Eds.). (2021). *The secret life of English-medium instruction in higher education: Examining microphenomena in context*, Routledge.

Borro, I., & Scolaro, S. (2021). Optimal and appropriate input in a second language: The potential of (modified-)elaborated input in distance and classroom learning. *E-JournALL, EuroAmerican Journal of Applied Linguistics and Languages, 8*(2), 53–69. doi:10.21283/2376905X.14.246

Borsetto, E., & Bier, A. (2021). Building on international good practices and experimenting with different teaching methods to address local training needs: The academic lecturing experience. *Alicante Journal of English Studies, 34*, 107–130.

Bowles, H., & Murphy, A. (Eds.). (2020). *English-medium instruction and the internationalization of universities*. Palgrave Macmillan.

Carrió-Pastor, M. L., & Bellés-Fortuño, B. (2021). (Eds.), *Teaching language and content in multicultural and multilingual classrooms CLIL and EMI approaches*. Palgrave MacMillan.

Chiasson, K., Terras, K., & Smart, K. (2015). Faculty perceptions of moving a face-to-face course to online instruction. *Journal of College Teaching & Learning (TLC), 12*(3), 321–240.

Cicillini, S., & Giacosa, A. (2020a). Online English-medium instruction (EMI) classes. What we have learned so far. In G. Adorni, A. Lorenzo, L. De Manzoni, & E. Medvet (Eds.), *Atti Convegno Nazionale DIDAMATiCA* (pp. 178–185) AICA - Associazione Italiana per l'Informatica ed il Calcolo Automatico.

Cicillini, S., & Giacosa, A. (2020b). Communication and interaction from face-to-face to online EMI degree programmes in the students' perspective – a case study. *EDEN Conference Proceedings, 1*, 422–432. doi:10.38069/edenconf-2020-rw0047

Conti, S. (2021). Didattica delle lingue a distanza durante l'emergenza Covid-19: il quadro generale. *E-JournALL, EuroAmerican Journal of Applied Linguistics and Languages, 8*(2), 9–52. doi:10.21283/2376905X.14.246

Coonan, C. M. (2012). *La lingua straniera veicolare*. UTET.

Costa, F. (2016). *CLIL (Content and language integrated learning) through English in Italian higher education*. LED.

Costa, F., & Mariotti, C. (2021). Strategies to enhance comprehension in EMI Lectures: Examples from the Italian context. In D. Lasagabaster & A. Doiz (Eds.), *Language use in English-medium instruction at university: International Perspectives on Teacher Practice* (pp. 80–99). Routledge.

Crawford Camiciottoli, B., & Fortanet-Gómez, I. (2015). *Multimodal analysis in academic settings: From research to teaching*. Routledge.

Dimova, S., & Kling, J. (Eds.). (2020). *Integrating content and language in multilingual universities*. Springer.

Dörnyei, Z. (2007). *Research methods in applied linguistics*. Oxford University Press.

Duff, P. (2008). *Case study research in applied linguistics*. Routledge.

Fedeli, M. (2018). The student voice in higher education and the implications of promoting faculty development. In V. Boffo & M. Fedeli (Eds.), *Employability and competences. Innovative curricula for new professions* (pp. 25–37). Firenze University Press.

Fortanet-Gómez, I., & Ruiz-Madrid, N. (2014). Multimodality for comprehensive communication in the classroom: Questions in guest lectures. *Ibérica, 28*, 203–224.

Gazdag, E., Nagy, K., & Szivák, J. (2019). "I spy with my little eyes . . ." The use of video stimulated recall methodology in teacher training – The exploration of aims, goals and methodological characteristics of VSR methodology through systematic literature review. *International Journal of Educational Research, 95*, 60–75.

Giacosa, A. (2021). Clarification and repair in emergency remote EFL classes. *E-JournALL – EuroAmerican Journal of Applied Linguistics and Languages, 8*(2), 161–184. doi:10.21283/2376905X.14.252

Hopkyns, S. (2022). Cultural and linguistic struggles and solidarities of Emirati learners in online classes during the COVID-19 pandemic. *Policy Futures in Education, 20*(4), 451–468. doi:10.1177/14782103211024815

Lasagabaster, D. & Doiz, A. (Eds.). (2021). *Language use in English-medium instruction at university: International Perspectives on teacher practice*. Routledge.

Lin, S-L., Wen, T-H., Ching, G., & Huang, Y-C. (2021). Experiences and challenges of an English as a medium of instruction course in Taiwan during COVID-19. *International Journal of Environmental Research and Public Health, 18*, 12920. doi:10.3390/ijerph182412920

Macaro, E., Akincioglu, M., & Han, S. (2020). English medium instruction in higher education: Teacher perspectives on professional development and certification. *International Journal of Applied Linguistics, 30*(1), 144–157.

Martin, F., Ahlgrim-Delzell, L., & Budhrani, K. (2017). Systematic review of two decades (1995 to 2014) of research on synchronous online learning. *American Journal of Distance Education, 31*(1), 3–19.

Morell, T. (2018). Multimodal competence and effective interactive lecturing. *System*, *77*, 70–79.

Morell, T. (2020). EMI teacher training with a multimodal and interactive approach: A new horizon for LSP specialists. *Language Value*, *12*(1), 56–87.

Paulsrud, B. A., Tian, Z., & Toth, J. (Eds.). (2021). *English-medium instruction and translanguaging*. Multilingual Matters.

Pun, J., Curle, S., & Yuksel, D. (Eds.). (2022). *The use of technology in English medium education*. Springer.

Querol-Julián, M. (2021). How does digital context influence interaction in large live online lectures? The case of English-medium instruction. *European Journal of English Studies*, *25*(3), 297–315.

Querol-Julián, M., & Crawford Camiciottoli, B. (2019). The impact of online technologies and English medium instruction on university lectures in international learning contexts: A systematic review. *ESP Today*, *7*(1), 2–23.

Quick, E. (2021). Aligning policy and practice: Linguistic and pedagogical strategies for the EMI classroom. In L. Mastellotto & R. Zanin (Eds.), *EMI and beyond: Internationalising higher education curricula in Italy* (pp. 53–76). Bozen University Press.

Rubio-Alcalà, F., & Coyle, D. (Eds.). (2021). *Developing and evaluating quality bilingual practices in higher education*. Multilingual Matters.

Ruiz Madrid, N., & Valeiras-Jurado, J. (2020). Developing multimodal communicative competence in emerging academic and professional genres. *International Journal of English Studies*, *20*(1), 27–50.

Tai, K. W. H. (2021). Researching translanguaging in EMI classrooms. In J. K. H. Pun & S. Curle (Eds.), *Research methods in English medium instruction* (pp. 119–132). Routledge.

Yüksel, H. G. (2022). Remote learning during COVID-19: Cognitive appraisals and perceptions of English medium of instruction (EMI) students. *Education and Information Technologies*, *27*(1), 347–363.

Appendix
Questionnaire for Lecturers (Distributed in Italian)

Subject Lectures Taught Through the English Language

Dear professors,
You are invited to fill in this brief questionnaire regarding teaching your subject in English during the pandemic. Participation is voluntary and the questionnaire is completely anonymous. All the questions regard ONLY the courses that you teach in English (EMI – English as a Medium of Instruction). You have ONE WEEK for the completion of the questionnaire. Your participation is very important for research on EMI.
Many thanks for your contribution.
Time estimated for completion: 5 minutes

1. Age

   Choose one option
   25–34 years
   35–44 years
   45–54 years
   55–64 years
   65–70 years

2. Department/Faculty with which you are affiliated:

3. Which subjects do you teach in English?

4. How much EMI teaching experience did you have before this year:

   Choose one option
   Less than a year
   One year
   2–5 years
   More than 5 years

5. Have you ever undertaken training for EMI teaching?

   Choose one option
   Yes
   No

6. During the pandemic what have you used most?

   Choose one option
   Recorded lectures
   Synchronous video lectures
   Part of the lecture synchronous and another part asynchronous
   PowerPoint slides with comments

7. For every hour of face-to-face lecturing, how much time of online teaching have you carried out?

   One hour
   Between half and one hour
   Less than half an hour

8. In addition to lectures, what materials have you provided to students for the EMI lectures?

   For each item, choose one option (never; sometimes; often; always)
   Downloadable powerpoints
   Lecture booklet
   Follow-up articles
   Video links
   Nothing

9. The students have seemed to be

   Choose one of the following
   More attentive than in face-to-face classes
   Just as attentive as in class
   Attentive at times
   Very absent
   I can't tell

10. What methods of interaction with students have you used most?

    Tools external to the teaching platform.
    Tools internal to the platform, during the class (chat, polls, other).
    With live questions during class.
    Non-live, for example, through the teaching platform or forum with questions and answers.

11. Which of these instruments have you used in your EMI classes for the first time during the pandemic?

    Select all the options that apply
    Videoconferences (such as Zoom and Teams)
    Recorded lectures made available on the teaching platform
    Powerpoint presentations with audio comments in the slides
    Chat
    Forum
    Course blog
    Collaborative writing tools (like Google Docs)

12. Has the preparation time for online classes been different from that required for face-to-face classes?

    Choose one option
    Yes, more time
    No, the same
    Yes, less time

13. In terms of course content, the courses that you have taught online have been:

    Choose one option
    The same as face-to-face classes
    Adapted to new timing and quantity of content
    Completely different

14. Which of these presentation strategies have you used more during online teaching than in face-to-face teaching?

    For each item, choose one option (I do not use this strategy; Less than in F2F lectures; The same as before; More than in F2F lectures)
    Questions
    Examples
    Summaries
    Repetitions
    Definitions
    Gesture
    Video clips
    Polls or quizzes
    Lesson objectives presented for each class
    Group work

15. Regardless of the type of online delivery, have you had to change your English language teaching approach during COVID?

    Select all the options that apply.
    No
    Yes, I am much more explicit in my teaching
    Yes, I need to give clear instructions on how to use the materials and/or the exercises.
    Yes, I need to vary activities more
    Yes, I have to repeat myself often to make sure the message is clear because of not seeing face-to-face reactions
    Other (please write in the space)

16. What method have you found the most effective in EMI classes delivered online?

    Select all the options that apply.
    Engaging students by dividing them into groups to carry out exercises during the lecture
    Discussion-based teaching between students and instructors
    Teaching without structured interaction with students
    Engaging students by having them prepare oral presentations and projects for in-class presentation
    Other (please write in the space)

17. Not using the native language in lectures during online delivery:

    Choose one option.
    Has made no difference
    Has made me feel more comfortable
    The use of technology has taken the pressure off as far as this is concerned
    Has made me feel less comfortable
    Has seemed harder
    I have actually used a lot of Italian in my English lectures as well.

18. Have your English-taught classes during the pandemic been . . . ?

    More teacher-centred (frontal) than usual
    More interactive than usual
    The same

19. What have the positive aspects of your English-taught classes in the pandemic been? Select all the options that apply.

    I haven't had to worry about the class management required in F2F teaching
    No need to think about teaching spaces and travel expenses

The chance to improve my technical competence
The chance to innovate my teaching
The opportunity to have more time
Knowing that students can access my recorded lectures more than once
The students were more active in the online classes
Motivating students to use the Internet to search for information

20. What were the negative aspects?

    Select all the options that apply.
    Lack of interpersonal relationship with students
    A change for the worse in student behaviour (reduced participation and number of students, lack of motivation)
    A less positive teaching experience due to the forced use of unfamiliar technology
    Time spent studying the new platforms at the expense of focusing on content
    I did not find anything negative

21. How satisfied are you with the online teaching you have carried out?

    From 1–4 (1 = not at all; 4 = very satisfied)

9 Input in EMI
Trusting the Process and the Journey

Cristina Mariotti

Classrooms where an L2 is used to convey subject matter content are a privileged setting to reflect on the role played by language used as a medium of instruction in the teaching-learning process. As the contributions in this volume have shown, it is important to analyse the quality of the input produced since input itself is the *prime mover* of the whole process. Bearing in mind that effective input should be relevant, in addition to being comprehensible (Krashen, 1982), we believe that *relevance* can be considered as a guiding concept when investigating input, especially considering controversies on the role played by language in EMI settings (see Lasagabaster, 2022, pp. 14–23, for an extensive review). From a university policy point of view, higher education institutions see EMI as a positive phenomenon as they hold the widespread belief that EMI helps underpin the internationalisation process (Doiz et al., 2014). From a pedagogical/educational point of view, it has been argued that EMI can improve students' English proficiency without having any detrimental effect on content learning, as shown by studies that have compared the test results obtained by comparable groups of students who were taught the same content by the same lecturer (Costa & Mariotti, 2017a; Dafouz et al., 2014). So why should EMI be a controversial issue and what role does input play in the picture?

In order to clarify this point, it might be worth expanding on the implications of the acronym by addressing the difference between EMI and other types of L2-medium instruction such as CLIL and ICLHE (for an extensive discussion of EMI, see Lasagabaster, 2022; Macaro, 2018; Pecorari & Halmström, 2018). What these three acronyms share is the fact they refer to the teaching-learning of an academic discipline through the medium of a language that is not the L1 of the learners, and possibly, of the instructor either. At the same time, however, there are differences. EMI (English-Medium Instruction) is typically used to refer to tertiary educational settings where English is used to support internationalisation programmes. Even if

DOI: 10.4324/9781003258407-9

EMI is traditionally defined as "the use of the English language to teach academic subjects (other than English itself) in countries or jurisdictions where the first language of the majority of the population is not English" (Macaro et al., 2018), the present book adopts a broader perspective. We have considered EMI as any occurrence of tertiary instruction where English is the medium used to teach disciplinary content to non-native speakers of English, regardless of whether the wider context in which the teaching occurs is English-speaking or not (see for instance Basturkmen, 2018). Thus, in EMI, the language, English, is considered merely as a medium of instruction, and language learning is not explicitly declared as an objective (Aguilar, 2017). The CLIL (Content and Language Integrated Learning) acronym, on the other hand, was created in the European area to define an approach originally inspired mostly by research carried out in the context of Canadian immersion education. In Europe, CLIL has been seen as a means to achieve the plurilingualism advocated by the European Commission. In practice, CLIL differs from EMI primarily because it entails the use of any L2 as the medium of instruction, not just English, and because in CLIL the focus is traditionally on the learning of both language and content. As a matter of fact, learners in CLIL classrooms are assumed to acquire language at the same time as they acquire knowledge in the content area (Brinton et al., 1989; Wode, 1999). Initially used in primary and secondary educational settings, in the past decade, CLIL has sometimes been used also to refer to higher education settings. Finally, ICLHE (Integrating Content and Language in Higher Education), also coined in the European context (Wilkinson & Zegers, 2007), bears more similarities with CLIL than with EMI as both CLIL and ICLHE contain the words "content" and "language" and refer to the construct of the "integration" of the two elements. This stresses the fact that in CLIL and in ICLHE, objectives related to the acquisition of language and content are combined when teaching/learning a discipline through an additional language.

As can be seen, the three acronyms all contain reference to language in one form or the other. Nevertheless, in tertiary education, stakeholders seem to be focusing mainly, and sometimes exclusively, on content learning, tending to overlook the relevance of L2 formal features and the development of the students' L2 competence (Lasagabaster & Doiz, 2021; Rose, 2021). Even when they address language-related topics or metalinguistic comments, content lecturers do not see themselves as English language teachers (Block & Moncada-Comas, 2022), a view shared by the students themselves (Block, 2021). At the same time, though, it is undeniable that even if language teaching and learning may not be an explicitly declared goal of EMI, content lecturers are still invested with the task of helping their students develop disciplinary literacy since "it is a fallacy to think that content and language can be separated in this way – content and language are inextricably entwined" (Airey, 2016, p. 93).

We can therefore say that in EMI linguistic input definitely matters, but it still represents uncharted territory when it comes to defining the degree of attention that the teaching and learning of the English language should receive since researchers are often confronted with a paradox. On the one hand, lecturers are concerned and aware of the challenges posed by the use of an L2 as the medium of instruction, but on the other, English is almost invisible, and competence in English tends to be taken for granted by higher education institutions, even if students often still struggle with the use of Academic English as the medium of instruction. Lasagabaster (2022) has observed that

> Even in the Nordic countries, whose students always achieve top positions in surveys on English competence, undergraduates find difficulties when tackling academic English. This is due to the fact that the linguistic resources they acquire extramurally or at grassroots level (the social presence of English is large: for example, films and TV series are not dubbed) differ considerably from the academic English they have to face in EMI courses.
>
> (p. 17)

We believe the main aim and rationale of this book has been to put language fully back into the picture in these settings. This work has tried to fulfil its mission by drawing on both empirical and theoretical studies which have addressed written and spoken input in several geographical areas using diversified methodological designs and instruments. We believe the contributions provide us with a multifaceted account of why and how the input produced in EMI settings should be considered relevant. This concluding chapter will focus on the pedagogical implications of the book and on future research directions in the hope this will assist both trainers and content lecturers engaging in lecturer training programmes.

Some Conclusions and Future Research Indications

One of the main facets the contributing authors agree on is the relevance of interaction and the occasions it poses to advance L2 competence and at the same time develop better content. Aintzane Doiz and David Lasagabaster investigated the role of teacher-led questions to promote productive thinking, highlighting the importance of asking open questions since these are cognitively demanding and promote critical thinking. The pedagogical implications of their chapter are particularly relevant for lecturer training, where special focus should be placed on making lecturers more aware of the importance of question-asking and the practice of interaction-fostering strategies that can increase student engagement.

Helen Basturkmen and Jiye Hong investigated lecturer–student exchanges occurring within EMI classrooms from the point of view of the incidental acquisition of vocabulary during language-related episodes (LREs), stressing the importance of meaningful interaction for learning vocabulary. These contributions remind us of how important it is to encourage EMI lecturers to reflect on the interaction patterns that arise during their lessons and to make them aware that, by fostering student self-selection, they provide them with more opportunities to produce output. By producing output, students can test their hypotheses about the foreign language. Moreover, output production can bring about improvements in accuracy and precision because learners are stimulated to process the L2 more intensely (with more mental effort) as they move from its semantic to its syntactic processing (Kowal & Swain, 1997; Swain, 2005). Finally, getting students to interact more in class can stimulate them to negotiate for meaning (Long, 1996); EMI contexts lend themselves particularly well to the development of negotiation sequences and scaffolding since students are assessed on the basis of their content knowledge, and it is likely they will be more motivated to communicate about their comprehension problems when initiating negotiation sequences even in teacher-led classrooms.

Cristina Mariotti's chapter investigated the characteristics of spoken input from a cross-disciplinary perspective, arguing that input modification strategies like signposting, redundancy expressed through repetitions, paraphrases and examples, a higher degree of interactivity, and a slower speech rate are more likely to make input more comprehensible when an L2 is used as the medium of instruction. At the same time, the emergence of specific, discipline-related strategies, such as the use of recurring metaphors, shows us that the EMI lecture is the space where teaching methodology and disciplinary literacy intersect and lecturers can deploy input presentation strategies tailored to increase students' awareness and the construction of disciplinary knowledge by adopting a student-centred approach.

Cynthia Pimentel Velázquez, Carmen Ramos Ordóñez and Víctor Pavón Vázquez examined the language component in teaching materials from a student-centred perspective. Starting from the premise that teaching materials are the observable component of pedagogy and fundamental to the development of academic literacy, the authors stressed the importance of adapting them to the subject-specific disciplines and settings students will be required to engage in while fostering motivation and student participation in the process.

Dario Banegas' chapter also deals with the creation of materials suitable for the EMI classroom based on the awareness that language and content are intertwined and their interplay can be exploited to the advantage of learners. In the author's view, the development of EMI materials should cater to the development of deep cognitive processes through the promotion of language and content scaffolding.

Monica Clua and Natalia Evnitskaya provide an insightful account of the interplay between interaction, roles and identity in the EMI classroom by showing us how interaction can lend itself to epistemic trespassing, a concept deriving from an imbalance between language proficiency and content knowledge between lecturers and students. This chapter reminds us that participants' roles can mingle and boundaries dissolve, leading them to co-construct subject matter discourse in ways that are at times unexpected.

Finally, Francesca Costa and Olivia Mair analyse students' engagement during online teaching, showing that students tend to be more reluctant to engage in online lessons with respect to face-to-face ones, and that lecturers should cater to students' participation, adapting their methodology by focusing on group work and interaction despite technological constraints. Costa and Mair's chapter converges with the other contributions in this book to remind EMI stakeholders of the importance of developing lecturer awareness. The linguistic and pedagogical choices of professors can have a high impact on the students' learning process, and it is fundamental to take these into consideration when designing effective training courses for EMI lecturers.

The chapters of this book are connected by a *leitmotif* which we believe can be summed up by saying that in EMI the relevance of input can be expressed in several different ways. Input matters in terms of both its quantity and its quality, and for both sides involved in the communicative event. It matters not only for the students, who benefit from the input, but also for the lecturers, who are responsible for producing most of the input students are exposed to in the form of spoken discourse and materials. Adopting the criterion of relevance as a guiding principle, we can develop hypotheses regarding the areas that EMI researchers should continue investigating using two metaphors: by viewing the production of input in EMI lectures both as a process and as a journey.

When considering input as the result of a process, stress falls on the importance of interaction. As pointed out by several contributors in this book, interaction can be used to co-construct input that is more comprehensible and salient. Its salience derives especially from the fact that input produced during lecturer–student interactions is more likely to contain repetitions, extensions, reformulations, rephrasings and expansions which immediately follow learner utterances and maintain reference to their meaning (Long, 1996,

p. 452). Moreover, the input produced by the lecturer while interacting with students has a greater likelihood of being noticed, and therefore acquired and later reused, by students (Mariotti, 2007, p. 61). Making lectures more dialogic also implies adopting a more student-centred approach, which consists in a "process of decentering of the focus of pedagogic action from the instructor to the students, giving the latter a much more predominant space during the class" (Cots, 2013, p. 117). This implies that lecturers can also become more aware of the difficulties of their students, who generally express a positive attitude towards EMI (Costa & Mariotti, 2017b; Doiz et al., 2019), while at the same time reporting difficulties on several levels. Students tend to find productive skills particularly challenging, including pronunciation and the use of subject-specific vocabulary (Doiz, Lasagabaster & Pavón, 2019).

Adopting a more interactive style and a student-centred perspective may also lead to student-led negotiation sequences. Among repair trajectories, negotiation of meaning has been recognised as having special status by the interactionist line of Second Language Acquisition (SLA) research, mainly represented by Michael Long and the Interaction Hypothesis (Gass, 2003; Long, 1996; Pica, 1994). Negotiation of meaning can be defined as a repair trajectory carried out by conversational participants to overcome communicative obstacles or prevent them from arising (Long & Robinson, 1998). Negotiation of meaning promotes L2 acquisition by leading the more competent speaker to modify the input in ways that can assist interlanguage development and by providing negative feedback at moments in conversation when learners are vested in the exchange, and therefore more likely to increase their level of attention. Moreover, it has been observed that in educational settings where emphasis is given to the content taught rather than the code used to convey it, and where learners are evaluated on the basis of their knowledge of the content rather than the accuracy of their linguistic production, learners may feel free to subvert the unspoken rules that govern classroom interactions and initiate negotiation sequences even in frontal teaching mode to make sure they have understood the subject matter content presented during the lesson (Basturkmen and Hong in this book; Pavesi, 2002, p. 52). Student-initiated negotiation sequences can lead the lecturer to produce input that is particularly geared towards the learning needs of the students, and during these sequences, both parties can effectively contribute to an input co-construction process that can lead to the production of input tailored to the specific needs of that specific set of students.

Notwithstanding the relevance of interaction sequences in producing tailored input, research has shown that EMI lectures are not characterised by a high degree of interactivity. Costa and Coleman (2013) found that the introduction of EMI in Italian HE apparently had not led to any change in the teaching style, with 71% of the respondents affirming that lecturers' monologues still constituted the most common form of content delivery. Similarly, Doiz and Lasagabaster (2021) observed that in many EMI contexts, lectures are still mainly monologic with the exception of short exchanges of a few words or short sentences. Therefore, we believe it is important to keep investigating the effects of interaction on the input production process and to promote professional development training that incorporates interaction-fostering strategies. Moreover, teacher training geared towards fostering interaction should also encourage lecturers to work on their pronunciation, which is often seen by lecturers as one of the biggest challenges in their teaching (Doiz et al., 2019).

By considering input production as being part of a journey, we focus on gathering information on the biography and experience of lecturers to acquire greater insight into their motivational systems. We already know a lot about the external forces that play a paramount role in the implementation of EMI experiences (e.g. the struggle to keep up with university rankings, the need to obtain visibility within one's own institution and the pressure to support the internationalisation process); however, to achieve a better understanding of the mechanism that shapes input production, it is also fundamental to investigate and encourage lecturers to focus on the internal motivational systems that drive their practice. Their attitudes and beliefs about English and teaching in English can have a great impact on how they teach. We know that teaching in English is not just about switching the language of instruction, and that an adaptation of teaching methodology is required (Ball & Lindsay, 2013) in addition to more time for preparation of materials and a greater effort in conveying content in an L2 (Thøgersen & Airey, 2011). However, we also know that lecturers surveyed in EMI research often talk about difficulties in developing self-confidence and finding their own *voice* when they are teaching in English. For these reasons, by working on the motivational system (Dörnyei, 2009; Dörnyei & Kubanyiova, 2014; Doiz & Lasagabaster, 2018) of lecturers and by also incorporating awareness-raising activities, research-informed professional development training might enable lecturers to select and apply input presentation strategies that are more in tune with their voice since those are the strategies they would most easily adopt and incorporate in their teaching. This line of research, which has recently received increased attention, should keep investigating the reflective practice of lecturers, which "involves EMI teachers systematically looking at what they do, how they do it, why they do it, what the outcomes are in terms of student learning, and what actions EMI teachers will take as a result of knowing all of this information" (Farrell, 2020, p. 277).

In light of these considerations, we can conclude that, in addition to considering input as a linguistic *object*, it might be necessary to see input in

EMI also as a *process* and as the result of the lecturers' experience, or the *journey* they undertake while teaching their disciplines in English. Ultimately, the relevance of input lies in the here and now of the classroom and the stakeholders that participate in its construction, which is why it is important to continue researching the features of EMI input in context. Therefore, as researchers, let us continue the journey and keep investigating and trusting the process.

References

Aguilar, M. (2017). Engineering lecturers' views on CLIL and EMI. *International Journal of Bilingual Education and Bilingualism, 20*(6), 722–735.

Airey, J. (2016). EAP, EMI or CLIL? In K. Hyland & P. Shaw (Eds.), *The Routledge handbook of English for academic purposes* (pp. 71–83). Routledge.

Ball, P., & Lindsay, D. (2013). Language demands and support for English-medium instruction in tertiary education. Learning from a specific context. In A. Doiz, D. Lasagabaster, & J. M. Sierra (Eds.), *English-medium instruction at universities. Global challenges* (pp. 44–66). Multilingual Matters.

Basturkmen, H. (2018). Dealing with language issues during subject teaching in EMI: The perspectives of two accounting lecturers. *TESOL Quarterly, 52*(3), 692–700.

Block, D. (2021). Emergent STEM lecturer identities: The shaping effects of EMI in action in an internationalised and Englishised HE context. *Language Teaching, 54*(3), 388–406.

Block, D., & Moncada-Comas, B. (2022). English-medium instruction in higher education and the ELT gaze: STEM lecturers' self-positioning as NOT English language teachers. *International Journal of Bilingual Education and Bilingualism, 25*(2), 401–417.

Brinton, D. M., Snow, A. M., & Wesche, M. B. (1989). *Content-based second language instruction*. Newbury House.

Costa, F., & Coleman, J. A. (2013). A survey of English-medium instruction in Italian higher education. *International Journal of Bilingual Education and Bilingualism, 16*(1), 3–19.

Costa, F., & Mariotti, C. (2017a). Differences in content presentation and learning outcomes in English-medium instruction (EMI) vs. Italian-medium instruction (IMI) contexts. In J. Valcke & R. Wilkinson (Eds.), *Integrating content and language in higher education* (pp. 187–204). Peter Lang.

Costa, F., & Mariotti, C. (2017b). Students' reception of English-medium instruction in three Italian universities. In C. Boggio & A. Molino (Eds.), *English in Italy: Linguistic, educational and professional challenges* (pp. 160–181). FrancoAngeli.

Cots, J. M. (2013). Introducing English-medium instruction at the University of Leida, Spain: Intervention, beliefs and practices. In A. Doiz, D. Lasagabaster, & J. M. Sierra (Eds.), *English-medium instruction at universities. Global challenges* (pp. 106–130). Multilingual Matters.

Dafouz, E., Camacho, M., & Urquia, E. (2014). "Surely they can't do as well": A comparison of business students' academic performance in English-medium and Spanish-as-first-language-medium programmes. *Language and Education, 28*, 223–236.

Doiz, A., Costa, F., Lasagabaster, D., & Mariotti, C. (2019). Linguistic demands and language assistance in EMI courses: What is the stance of Italian and Spanish Undergraduates? *Lingue e Linguaggi, 33*, 69–85.

Doiz, A., & Lasagabaster, D. (2018). Teachers' and students' second language motivational self system in English-medium instruction: A qualitative approach. *TESOL Quarterly, 52*(3), 657–679.

Doiz, A., & Lasagabaster, D. (2021). Analysing EMI teachers' and students' talk about language and language use. In D. Lasagabaster & A. Doiz (Eds.), *Language use in English-medium instruction at university: International perspectives on teacher practice* (pp. 34–55). Routledge.

Doiz, A., Lasagabaster, D., & Pavón, V. (2019). The integration of language and content in English-medium instruction courses: Lecturers' beliefs and practices. *Ibérica, 38*, 151–175.

Doiz, A., Lasagabaster, D., & Sierra, J. (2014). Language friction and multilingual policies at higher education: The stakeholders' view. *Journal of Multilingual and Multicultural Development, 35*(4), 345–360.

Dörnyei, Z. (2009). The L2 motivational self system. In Z. Dörnyei & E. Ushioda (Eds.), *Motivation, language identity and the L2 self* (pp. 9–42). Multilingual Matters.

Dörnyei, Z., & Kubanyiova, M. (2014). *Motivating learners, motivating teachers: Building vision in the language classroom*. Cambridge University Press.

Farrell, T. S. C. (2020). Professional development through reflective practice for English-medium instruction (EMI) teachers. *International Journal of Bilingual Education and Bilingualism, 23*(3), 277–286.

Gass, S. M. (2003). Input and interaction. In C. Doughty & M. H. Long (Eds.), *Handbook of second language acquisition* (pp. 224–255). Blackwell.

Kowal, M., & Swain, M. (1997). From semantic to syntactic processing: How can we promote it in the immersion classroom? In R. K. Johnson & M. Swain (Eds.), *Immersion education: International perspectives* (pp. 284–309). Cambridge University Press.

Krashen, S. (1982). *Principles and practice in second language acquisition*. Pergamon.

Lasagabaster, D. (2022). *English-medium instruction in higher education*. Cambridge University Press.

Lasagabaster, D., & Doiz, A. (Eds.). (2021). *Language use in English-medium instruction at university: International perspectives on teacher practice*. Routledge.

Long, M. H. (1996). The role of linguistic environment in second language acquisition. In W. C. Ritchie & T. K. Bhatia (Eds.), *Handbook of second language acquisition* (pp. 413–468). Academic Press.

Long, M. H., & Robinson, P. (1998). Focus on form. Theory, research, and practice. In C. Doughty & J. Williams (Eds.), *Focus on form in classroom second language acquisition* (pp. 15–41). Cambridge University Press.

Macaro, E. (2018). *English medium instruction*. Oxford University Press.
Macaro, E., Curle, S., Pun, J., An, J., & Dearden, J. (2018). A systematic review of English medium instruction in higher education. *Language Teaching*, *51*(1), 36–76.
Mariotti, C. (2007). *Interaction strategies in English-medium instruction*. FrancoAngeli.
Pavesi, M. (2002). Per una didattica naturale: strategie discorsive nell'insegnamento integrato di lingua e contenuti. In F. Maggi, C. Mariotti, & M. Pavesi (Eds.), *Lingue straniere veicolo di apprendimento* (pp. 47–64). Ibis.
Pecorari, D., & Halmström, H. (2018). At the crossroads of TESOL and English medium instruction. *TESOL Quarterly*, *52*(3), 497–515.
Pica, T. (1994). Research on negotiation: What does it reveal about second-language learning conditions, processes and outcomes? *Language Learning*, *44*, 493–527.
Rose, H. (2021). Students' language-related challenges of studying through English: What EMI teachers can do. In D. Lasagabaster & A. Doiz (Eds.), *Language use in English-medium instruction at university: International perspectives on teacher practice* (pp. 145–166). Routledge.
Swain, M. (2005). The output hypothesis: Theory and research. In E. Hinkel (Ed.), *Handbook on research in second language learning and teaching* (pp. 471–483). Lawrence Erlbaum Associates.
Thøgersen, J., & Airey, J. (2011). Lecturing undergraduate science in Danish and in English: A comparison of speaking rate and rhetorical style. *English for Specific Purposes*, *30*(3), 209–221.
Wilkinson, R., & Zegers, V. (Eds.). (2007). *Researching content and language integration in higher education*. Maastricht University Language Centre.
Wode, H. (1999). Incidental vocabulary acquisition in the foreign language classroom. *Studies in Second Language Acquisition*, *21*(2), 243–258.

Index

Note: Page numbers in *italics* indicate a figure and page numbers in **bold** indicate a table on the corresponding page.

academic literacy 62, 88, 93, 94, 119
agentive actions 67, 68, 72, 74, 77
agentic capacity 67, 75
Applied Linguistics/English Linguistics 3
applied linguists 2
authentic language 57
authentic materials 55, 83
authentic sources of input 86
authentic texts 3, 56
autonomous learning 84

Basic Interpersonal Communication Strategies (BICS) 56
BICS *see* Basic Interpersonal Communication Strategies

Cognitive Academic Language Proficiency (CALP) 56, 57
Categorization Analysis 70
classroom, student-teacher agency in 66–78; agency and 67; agentive actions in 67; general English language knowledge reflected in 68; epistemic authority, epistemic progression at stake in 77; facilitating interactions with students in 77; Membership Categorisation Analysis applied to 8, 70, 76–77;

Positioning Analysis applied to 8, 70; shared understanding negotiated in 68; specific disciplinary discourse knowledge in English and 67–68;
classroom discourse 36; role of questions in 13–14; *see also* questioning; questions
classroom interaction 28, 30, 32, 35, 36–37;
CLIL *see* Content and Language Integrated Learning
codeswitching 5, 105
coding 32; first-cycle and second-cycle 104; initial and axial 86
coding conventions 24
collocations 29
Common European Framework of Reference for Languages 15
common language proficiency 54
Content and Language Integrated Learning (CLIL) 54; characteristics of effective materials for 56–57;
content, language as 57
conversational language 56
conversational participants 121
Conversation Analysis (CA) 8, 69, 76

disciplinary collocations 35
disciplinary content 6

Index

disciplinary cultures 15
disciplinary discourse: EMI and 8, 40–49
disciplinary languages and literacy 41, 48, 54, 117, 119;
disciplinary variation of discourse features 36

EAP *see* English for Academic Purposes
EFL *see* English as a Foreign Language
EMI *see* English-Medium Instruction
English as a Foreign Language (EFL) 85, 98
English for Academic Purposes (EAP) in Oman 85
English language proficiency 49, 82, 116
English-Medium Instruction (EMI): disciplinary discourse and 8, 40–49; EMI/CLIL 54–58, 61–62; input in 1–9, 116–123; as journey 123; materials development 82–94; multimodal analysis of student-teacher agency in classroom 66–78; online 98–100; as process 123
English-taught courses at universities: materials design for development of subject-specific literacies in 53–62
epistemic authority of teacher 66–69, 76
epistemic progression 77–78
epistemic trespassing 68, 120
epistemological appropriateness 41
epistemological beliefs: knowledge structures and 47
epistemology 49
European Commission 117
explicitness 42, 43–47, 49, 56, 61
explicit requests 20
explicit technique: input enhancement as 6

formulaic sequences 27, 29, 32, 35
framework for the analysis of vocabulary language-related episodes (LREs) 8, 26–37; application of 32; framing 14, 19, 22

graphic organisers, use of 88, *89*

ICLHE *see* Integrating Content and Language in Higher Education
incidental attention to vocabulary 26, 36, 37
incidental language learning 3, 6
incidental vocabulary acquisition 28–29, 119
input: asynchronous 85; comprehensible 2–3; in EMI 1–9, 116–123; explicitness in 43–44; intentional 7; interaction with 44–45; linguistic 42; of linguistically K- content/ K+ teacher 76, 77; lecturer 87, 102; lexical 98; as linguistic object 122; non-interactive 6; online 9, 97–108; online EMI 98–100; oral 105; as process 123; relevance of 2, 120, 123; spoken 8, 40–49; student-centred teaching and 45–47; written 8
input enhancement 4, 6
Input Hypothesis 4–5
input presentation strategies 5, 41, 46; discipline-specific 47–48
input studies: relevance of 3–6
Integrating Content and Language in Higher Education (ICLHE) 82, 94, 116, 117
interactional studies 69
Interaction Hypothesis 5, 121
interaction 5, 7, 14; case study of one student-teacher interaction 69, 70–76; class/classroom 27, 28, 30, 32, 35, 36–37; collaboratively mediated 83; disciplinary classroom 26; English-taught lectures and 44–45; facilitating interaction with students 77; institutional 66; meaning as modified interaction 3;

meaning-making 13; mediated by social categories 70; online EMI 99–101, 103, 105–108; SLA–EMI 2; social 67; socio-interactional methodologies 66, 68; teacher/student class interaction 15, 16–19, 20, 23; turn-by-turn generated identities in and for interaction 70; *see also* classroom interaction
interactional studies 69
interaction-fostering strategies 45, 46, 49, 119, 122
interaction sequences 42, 118, 121
interactionist line of SLA research 121
Italian higher education/universities 44, 47, 51, 100, 102
Italian native speakers 44, 46, 47
Italian teaching in EMI *see* online input

knowledge progression 68

language-related episodes (LREs): framework for the analysis of vocabulary *30*; sub-types of form-focused LREs by discipline **34**; sub-types of lexical choice-focused LREs by discipline **34**; sub-types of meaning-focused LREs by discipline **33**; *see also* framework for the analysis of vocabulary language-related episodes (LREs)
learner-teacher 73; *see also* teacher-learner
lecturer awareness, importance of developing 8, 40–42, 47–48, 102, 120
lecturing 45–47; online 107; student-centred 46; video 108
linguicism 82

Membership Categorization Analysis 8, 70, 76
membership categories 74, 77

multimodal analysis 7; student-teacher agency in classroom 66–78
multimodal Conversation Analysis (CA) 70, 76; *see also* Conversation Analysis
multimodality in teaching 5, 22, 98, 99;
multimodal dynamics of discourse 69, 93
multimodal thinking 14, 21, 22;
multiple choice exercises 85
multisemiotic resources 99
multi-unit lexical units 35
multiword entities 29, 32, 33, **34**

online EMI input 9, 98–100
online input: EMI pedagogy and 9, 97–108, 120; 87; questionnaire for lecturers (Italian) regarding teaching during pandemic 111–115; simulated recall analysis during 104–107;
online learning/education 93, 94, 97, 106
online synchronous seminars 85
online teaching module 87; student-centred teaching and 45–47

paraphrasis 5
plurilingualism 117
pluriliteracies 57
Positioning 70, 76
prime mover 1, 2, 116

Q-DRESS 44
question-based prelude 14, 22–23
questioning: approaches and strategies 16, 19–20, 23;
questioning exchanges (activity), role of 13
questions 7; dialogic 14; role in classroom discourse 13–20; reformulation of 18; semantic tapestry 14, 19, 21; Socratic questioning 14, 19–20; 22–23;

Index 129

teacher-led/teacher-fronted questioning 14, 15, **17**, 22, 23, 118; verbal jigsaw 14, 19–20

reading materials 26, 60
reformulating/reformulation 5, 24, 44, 60, 72, 105, 120;
rehabilitation of input *see* input
relevance: of disciplinary languages 55; as guiding concept 116; of input/input studies 2, 3–7, 120, 123; of interaction/interaction sequences 118, 121; of L2 formal features 117; of language linked to subject content 54; of redundancy 42
repair sequence 68, 72, 77
repair trajectory 121
ROAD-Mapping 3

sociocultural theory perspective on 83
scaffolding strategies 84
scaffolding through attention to disciplinary literacy 88–92
scaffolding through localisation 92–94
secondary education settings 37
Second Language Acquisition (SLA) 1, 4–6, 27, 98;
semantic clarity 44
semantics 85, 119
semantic tapestry 14, 19, 21
semantic transparency 29
Socratic questioning 14, 19–20
student-centered teaching 45–47, 100

student comments 105
student engagement with learning 87, 93, 98–100; increasing 119; lecturer's perceptions of 103; online learning and 87, 98–100, 103, 105, 120
SVL *see* synchronous videoconferencing lectures
synchronous videoconferencing lectures (SVL) 99, 103

teacher-as-expert 66
teacher-fronted lectures/classroom 40–42, 45, 67, 119
teacher-learner 73
teacher-led/teacher-fronted questioning 14, 15, **17**, 22, 23, 118
teacher-student exchanges: role of productive thinking in 13–23; *see also* classroom discourse
teaching to a void 99

university lecture, oral tradition of 66
university rankings 122

verbal cloze 14, 20
verbal jigsaw 14, 19–20
video-based activity 90
video-recorded classes 24
voice variation 107

zone of proximal development (ZPD) 83

For Product Safety Concerns and Information please contact our EU
representative GPSR@taylorandfrancis.com
Taylor & Francis Verlag GmbH, Kaufingerstraße 24, 80331 München, Germany